Unseen Arms
Reaching Out

by

AMY BROOKS

WITH

Jeff Ferris

I hope you are
blessed by Amy's story

colossians 3:23,24

Unseen Arms Reaching Out

by Amy Brooks
with Jeff Ferris

Published by:

Joshua Tree Publishing
• Chicago •

JoshuaTreePublishing.com

ISBN13-Digit: 978-1-941049-38-9
Photo Credits are listed in About the Authors, page 263.
Printed in the United States of America

Scripture Copyrights:

Disclaimer:

DEDICATION

I dedicate this book to my wonderfully
supportive parents,

Rich and Janet Brooks

Foreword

I can do all things through Christ who strengthens me.
Philippians 4:13 (NKJV)

by Brett Barry

I 've wrestled with the practicality of this *Bible* quote for many years. It was written by a guy who had an encounter with the risen Christ that initially made him blind, yet ultimately made him see. Before meeting Jesus, he knew only his own ambitions, flowing fervently out of what he believed was right and good. Afterward, his eyes were opened to God's love and authority and, ultimately, to what God could do through a life yielded fully to Him. That revelation simultaneously broke him and mended him. Destroyed him and saved him. Stopped him dead in his tracks while compelling him to spend the rest of his life traveling the world to build up what he had previously tried to destroy.

The beauty of that kind of life-changing revelation is its long-term impact; not only upon the individual, but also upon those they meet.

Through music, I too have had the honor of traveling the world in support of the same gospel message the Apostle Paul served. While I love contributing things that build the Church, one of my favorite parts of each traveling adventure is meeting the people for whom I get to play as well as those along the way. Airports, trains, taxis, subways, city and small town streets...everyone has a story, and every story is unique. Every one counts because *everyone* counts.

While my life has been enriched by the life stories of many fascinating individuals, every so often I encounter someone that really stands out. Someone like Paul, who, at peace with God is at peace with himself. And that speaks. Powerfully.

In my experience, Amy Brooks is one of those stand-outs: At peace with God, at peace with herself.

Hopefully, you'll get the opportunity to meet her one day. When you do, I believe you'll understand what I'm talking about. At roughly 2' 6" tall, she stands head and shoulders above so many. Yep. Little, monumental, Amy. She doesn't like people gushing over her generous heart or her Christ-centered will of steel, so I won't do that. But as we launch into this next phase of her journey I would like to address something specific about her that, though available to all, few people actually have, for it challenges me deeply.

So, what is it about Amy that's so impacting? I've thought about this a lot over the past year since meeting her and her equally inspiring parents, Rich and Janet. It can be difficult to articulate in practical terms, for the process of personal growth looks different in each individual. But there is a core tell among the truly broken in Christ, one I see so strongly in Amy.

It's not that she has a physical handicap yet still manages to do so much. Her accomplishments are definitely impressive. Neither is it her positive attitude toward life or her unwavering determination and dedication to excel in a world designed for the abilities of others. These all speak volumes and are definitely part of its fruit, but it's something more. Something deeper.

It's more along the lines of, Amy helps remind me that, while there is a future that those who love God look forward to sharing with Him, the objective of our time on earth is as much about learning to embrace the journey as it is desiring the destination. It's about learning to see our hardships as opportunities to grow in character and, therefore, being thankful for the process as much as the end result. It's about knowing so well the God in which we hope that it shapes our perspective of each moment we're now living.

Jesus knew it: *My kingdom is not of this world... I only do what I see The Father doing. I do nothing on my own but speak just what the Father has taught me.*

Paul knew it: *Find out what pleases The Lord... that I might share in His sufferings... these light and momentary troubles.*

Amy knows it. *I am fearfully and wonderfully made...* (her life verse) Psalm 139:14-17 (NIV).

Wait! Fearfully and wonderfully made? Amy, how can you say that? Good grief, girl! Have you forgotten? You have no arms or legs!

But then, that's it! Did you catch it? That's the ticket. She knows God and trusts Him to the point of peaceful resolve.

She could be mad at God and bitter toward others, even toward life itself. But she isn't. And not because she's wired to be a happy-go-lucky person. She'll confirm she isn't that either. It's because she, in her faith journey, has come to know God well enough to trust not only what He directs in her life, but what He allows. As such, she's confident that He can best use her as she is. Does she have bad days where she might struggle with self-centered challenges? She has no arms or legs in a world designed for people with arms and legs, was abandoned at birth, suggested by a relative that she be left to die, expected by professionals to amount to nothing…

Yes, it's safe to say she has bad days.

But then…God.

While Amy is certainly as susceptible as any of us to faithlessness or self-centered failure, I believe her heart's pursuit is to remain focused upon God's goodness and His power to work within her. From that place, and by His strength, she then chooses to wrestle her perspective to one of thankfulness and honor to God regardless of how challenging life may be or how she may feel about it from time to time. In short, her confession is trustworthy because His affect upon her life perspective is clearly visible, in spite of the hand she's been dealt (no pun intended). Whenever I see that in someone, really give it some wait-for-it contemplation, it awakens and challenges me at my very core because it identifies how I want to be; more importantly, who I want to be: one who knows and trusts God to the point of thankful resolve—no matter what. It also reveals how much of me there is yet in the way.

You know, as I read over what I'm saying, it sounds as though I'm lifting Amy to some "Saintly" status. But then, as I think about it, I suppose I am. For, in Scripture, a saint is not someone who has arrived but one fully devoted to God and therefore engaged in the process of living for His glory—of becoming more like Him.

Hmm…Saint Amy. Yep, that works. *Sorry Amy, if that's too much just ignore that part! (NOTE: Jeff requested I write the Foreword as a surprise for Amy—so she didn't get to proof it.)*

Well, there it is. As you read Amy's story and get to know her, I hope you'll keep in mind her inner mission. Quick-witted, graciously sarcastic and in the pursuit of living fully yielded to God, she's a character, with character. A whole person even without limbs. After the initial impact of what one might perceive as limitation due to her seeming handicap comes the eventual realization that she's actually quicker, faster, taller and stronger in the things that count than most NBA or NFL stars are in their professions (add MMA if you like).

As Amy tells her story, she will help you find your center in God. Like an ounce of prevention, her perspective is worth a pound of cure. She will inspire you to reach beyond your current comfort zone to fully embrace the hardships of your own personal journey toward becoming a whole person, even if you do have arms and legs.

Thank you, Amy.

When those who seemingly cannot, somehow do, it reminds those of us who can just how much we must.

Dear reader, I encourage you to follow along on Amy's journey. May you be fully challenged and given to God. In the strength of Christ, you too can do all things.

Brett Barry
Singer/Songwriter/Christ Follower
Founder & Director, Inseparable Lives
Frederick, MD

I praise you because I am fearfully and wonderfully made; your works are wonderful, I know that full well.

My frame was not hidden from you when I was made in the secret place.

When I was woven together in the depths of the earth, your eyes saw my unformed body. All the days ordained for me were written in your book before one of them came to be.

How precious to me are your thoughts, O God!

Psalm 139:14-17 (NIV)

Reaching Out ~ OrphanCare Expo '14

Introduction

To Whom It May Concern

Dear Sir, Madam, or Anonymous Reader,

With my first book ending with a speech, it seemed fitting to begin my second with a letter. And then, we'll move on to another speech.

Well, not really an immediate speech, but sort of.

Maybe a road trip first.

This letter is not the chain type or of the "Dear John" variety. It isn't an impersonal, mechanical, computer-generated form letter, a published editorial, or a signed affidavit.

It's just a simple letter from me to you—written in Pittsburgh, printed in Chicago. It may have also made a quick stop along the way to visit some friends in Toledo, but it is to you, nevertheless. Consider it to be a handwritten invitation...without the hand, of course.

In fact, you might think of this entire book as such—an invitation to continue with me on this voyage called "life." As we go, I will address matters and concerns of my heart and soul.

I'll share things about me that you don't know and things about my family that you'll wish you didn't know.

Please, refrain from using flash photography. Recording devices are also prohibited. Most of the images and sounds within this book are likely too frightening to keep, anyhow.

That said, I trust that you have already begun this journey by reading part one of my story in the form of my first book, Unseen Arms. If not, it doesn't matter. I won't hold it against you. That isn't one of my concerns; don't allow it to be one of yours, either. You'll be brought up to speed in no time; I'm pretty easy to keep up with, after all. Come along regardless, right where you am and just how you is.

Pertaining to life in general—with or without working human limbs—we all live it to the tick of a clock and to the beat of a drum of one brand or another.

As for concerns, each of us has them. This book opens with some. Concerns come in a variety of shapes and fashions. Some are more intense and longer lasting than others. Many can become unbearable.

Some folks wear their concerns on their sleeves like Captain's stripes or merit badges. I no longer possess the monkey arms of my past; therefore, my sleeves are not long enough for that. Whenever visible, they don't allow me the ability or the convenience of such a display. If they did, I prefer to not wear negative emotions on them. It wouldn't be book worthy.

More importantly, it wouldn't be time worthy.

If my imaginary sleeves are to bear anything, I wish it to be the reality of my faith and not the show of concerns, which often prove to be unfounded and undeserving of mental occupation.

What do your sleeves bear? What are your concerns? Are they heavy? Is your life punctuated with worry? Is it saturated with fear?

I request the honor of your presence. Let's travel together through the pages of this book. It will be a lonely voyage without you.

I am confident that you'll find the best of my story is yet to come. There will be plenty of continued humor, better flesh wounds, an assortment of wonderful people, and so much more. There are a few friends, in particular, who I am greatly enthused about introducing.

Since the publishing of my first book, I have been doing some showing up and some reaching out. But I'm not the only one; others have also been doing the same. There will be an abundance of showing up and a variety of reaching out to read of in the following pages.

With my many new experiences and recent accomplishments, I do not consider the interval between my first book and this one to be marked as "time." We can think of it...well, possibly as "halftime."

That period has now passed.

The second half is ready to begin!

So, walk with me, if you will.

Waddle if you like.

Limp if you must.

Either way, you can slow to my pace without having to stoop to my level.

I think we are all in for a pleasant stroll together.

But first, we need to take that road trip. Dad will be driving while I share more of my story with you.

If you begin to feel stressed or concerned as we go, just take a deep breath in and let it out. And repeat if necessary.

All the while, whatever your preferred method of conveyance—whether we walk or stumble or glide or stroll—as we inch our way through this collection of chapters, I hope you will think of me as "your friend, always."

And I mean that, "sincerely."

~Amy

Table of Contents

Table of Contents (cont)

Part One

Now and Then

What lies behind us, and what lies before us are tiny matters compared to what lies within us.

~Ralph Waldo Emerson

1

Frozen In Time

Who'da thunk it? Who would've known? I mean how many people are truly aware that 3:00 a.m. really does exist? For people like Dad who served in the Army, it's equivalent to only like oh-three hundred hours or something!

Until this moment, I had only heard about it somewhere. Now here I am experiencing a personal encounter with the hideous thing.

Yes, Virginia, there really is a 3:00 a.m., and I have found it to be a long, tall serving of stink on a stick. Don't set your alarm to find out; just stay in bed, and take my word for it.

But why was this hour invented? And how is it considered "a.m.," thereby qualifying as "a morning?" Doesn't it meet the criteria of night? Yes, it does.

Do I look like I have eye shine or some type of natural night vision? No, I don't.

Unless this hour silently passes my home and continues onward in an orderly fashion while I remain in a deep, undisturbed sleep, I don't particularly like it, especially when it stops to rattle me awake.

Though I had already suspected that I wouldn't appreciate such an experience, I'm finding it to be quite true on this very morning.

The date is Friday, February 20, 2014.

Or is it still Thursday night, the 19th? Gahhh!

This is simply an unacceptable human business hour.

I can only hope it isn't habit forming.

Having been born on a Monday night, I'm not comprised of much early-Friday-morning material. And Friday starts the weekend, right? Isn't there some sort of rule that says we are required to sleep in on weekends?

We are all supposed to be in a sleep-induced coma right now—out cold, completely frozen over, in hibernation mode, dead to the world. But we're not.

I don't mean to discriminate, but 3:00 a.m. really isn't a protected class or a guarded time-slot. That said, I believe of all the hours on the clock, it should be completely banished.

Why is it there? More accurately, why is it *here* getting me up? Whose idea was 3:00 a.m., anyway? Why do we need it? And why should I ever have to awaken at this time?

I'm sorry for rambling. I'm sleepy. And I'm nervous because I have to head to Charlotte, North Carolina, to give a couple of public speeches. But can you understand my confusion? If you stay up till this hour, it's much too late. If you wake up now, it's way too early.

So, make up my mind already: is it late, or is it early?

Remembering my school years, 3:00 p.m. had always been a preferred reading of the clock on any given weekday. Now, these many years later—minus twelve hours—there's nothing appealing about these digits.

It's so dark outside that I won't even be able to see my hand in front of my face.

Wait…I also have that problem at high noon.

New Yorkers have that whole "city that never sleeps" thing going on. But what they do is their business. What happens in the Big Apple should stay there. The ways of their city shouldn't apply to anyone else.

I live in Pittsburgh. We do things differently by actually sleeping at night. As far as my body is concerned, 3:00 a.m. is nighttime, an hour for sleeping and nothing else. Otherwise, it's unfavorable to one's circadian rhythm and overall beauty requirements.

Simply put, Pennsylvanians need their beauty rest. At least I do. Besides, a 3:00 a.m. wakeup call was never mentioned anywhere in my travel brochure.

Making things especially miserable is the harsh feuding that's been going on outside, with Mother Nature and Old Man Winter refusing to behave themselves in an amicable fashion. I think Satan himself is egging them on.

For months, they've been throwing frozen punches, each blow landing squarely on the chins of everyone residing in cold weather regions such as mine. These unruly, tag-teaming forces schemed and conspired in vindictive accord to create a brew of horrible weather into which we now have to venture.

Additionally, I've feared that I'm being an imposition on good people who care about me. My parental units top that list.

Dad is being dragged out of retirement from his steel-hauling days to haul me 453 miles south. Mom's going also, to assist with my personal care…and to coach Dad on how to drive correctly.

Added to the stress of the travel itself are my worries of the countless things that might go wrong and my general nervousness of what the trip will require.

Call it "buyer's remorse."

Or "agreer's regret."

Or something.

Each ingredient—3:00 a.m., darkness, freezing rain, uncertainty—everything has awakened early and positioned itself to challenge us.

Also, it seems ironic that I came wrapped in a convenient travel size package, but it hasn't made traveling any more convenient for me or my traveling companions. It isn't as if they can just toss me into an overnight bag, though I'd probably fit okay.

Despite my cuddly size, expeditions of any kind have been made more difficult because of it—being encased inside a wheelchair and often hampered by snow, ice, mud, or other uncontrollable elements that prohibit free movement. With that aside, you are probably a lot like me.

In many ways—on both the mushy inside and on the crunchy exterior—we are likely all the same. We enjoy our warmth and comfort. We are often resistant to change. We prefer the smooth and familiar over that which is unknown or unpredictable. And who wouldn't much rather be dipped in honey and lowered into a pit of fire ants than go out and talk in public?

Ugh!

Given an all-out choice, or even a partial one, I'd rather do artwork. But only after finishing a good night's sleep inside my toasty warm bedcovers. Quiet midday art projects are simply what I'd choose over getting up to go out and give a speech.

I'm just a basic homebody.

Why wouldn't I be? Life's been good here.

Beneath this roof and within these walls, I've had everything I've ever needed—the love of family and friends, shelter, security, my *Bible*, and my dog. And let's not forget the practicalities of my own customized tinkletorium!

Of course, that's not to say I don't get out. I do. But when I must, or when I simply choose to, I prefer doing so under more suitable conditions.

To be clear about it, going out doesn't mean I want a personal jet or a luxury motor coach with rump-roasting seat heaters. Nor do I need a chauffeured limousine with its fancy driver rolling out a red carpet for me.

Dad has always done just fine in our van, getting me where I needed to go. As an added bonus, he usually sees to it that I get back home, too.

And that's where I prefer to be most of the time—home with the people I love and the activities I cherish.

There's no place like it. A girl named Dorothy made that clear, long ago. She was from Kansas. People sleep there also, especially at 3:00 a.m., I'm sure.

But I'm glad you're awake. Isn't it odd that we'd bump into each other at such an hour? Climb in and ride along with me. I have lots to share with you to help the miles pass more quickly.

Just be sure to bundle up; it's freezing outside.

2

Warm Weather Girl

Pittsburgh, Pennsylvania. It's the place of my birth, my rearing, and my residence. That's what I've always known. It is my normal, my familiar, my safe zone.

I have always been proud of my homeland. It does hold its own marque of earth-appeal with rugged beauty and subtle charm. But its monikers suggest nothing of direct or indirect sunlight or physical warmth, even if the sun is positioned directly overhead.

We are *The City of Bridges*. We have bridges straddling all over the place whether we need them or not. They've also thrown in a few tunnels just to mix things up a bit and make it more confusing for those who have to drive here.

There's nothing inherently cozy about any of that.

We are more commonly known as *The Steel City*. Most of those bridges are made of it. Yet, there just aren't enough working steel mills here anymore to sufficiently warm the air and land from October to April. And the heat that does find us in the warmer months is mostly absorbed into my sister, Myia, with her excessive sunbathing.

This is all of great significance to me because I haven't been winterized or weatherproofed in any way. That's why an early morning outing in February can be particularly traumatic for me. When it comes to cold weather, I am *such* a girl. And I've never felt stylish in long johns for some reason.

Don't get me wrong; I don't necessarily crave the extreme heat and steamy humidity that's found in a Miami summer—the kind that scorches your hair and melts your face—but I truly am a warm weather girl by nature and by choice.

It is greatly unfortunate that the climate in my region doesn't fully accommodate me on that preference. If our weather cycles were to offer an exclusive choice between sunburns and snotsicles, I'd take the sunburns. But what I really prefer is seventy degrees in the shade, thank you.

Concerning southern places like Florida, for example, I do appreciate the concept of natural warmth that lingers persistently. That's probably one of God's most impressive ideas. I suspect even He doesn't like winter a whole lot, which is why He shortened the month of February, deciding to just get it over with.

Even then, it seems everything comes with a catch, including this slightly abridged page on the calendar. If 3:00 a.m. isn't abnormal enough, a meager thirty-some hours into the month of February, my home state plays host to a peculiar ceremony that carries lots of local media hype and a load of national attention.

It happens only about eighty miles from our neighborhood, in a nor'easterly direction, in the town of Punxsutawney.

Groundhog's Day.

It's a lot like 3:00 a.m., meaning, *What's up with that?*

I'm sure even Bill Murray would agree.

Imagine such a celebrated event never being a day off school for us kids or a paid holiday for Dad. But all eyes and cameras are on it every year. More accurately, they all focus on a critter called Punxsutawney Phil.

From my perspective, the outcome is always predictable and never good. It all seems to be a set-up, in fact. Even when it's cloudy, there is such an overabundance of camera flashes and studio lighting that he'll see his shadow, regardless.

I'd like to know whose idea it was to allow a ground-dwelling rodent to decide how much longer our winters should be extended in the first place.

For him it's a pretty good gig, right?

Phil doesn't mind winter dragging out for another six weeks; he's covered in a layer of fur. And he's likely to return to hibernation and just spend that time sleeping. And I'd bet no one would dare wake him up at three in the morning.

Ending winter should be a human decision.

Perhaps we could put it to a vote.

I wouldn't mind venturing out into the cold to assume the responsibility. If I see a shadow of any type, it would be my immediate declaration that we have a mere six more minutes of winter, and it would be done.

Then again, when we humans try to form a solution for such things, we often don't think them through very well. Take the whole thing with Daylight Savings Time. Did someone really believe it would be of much help to speed up winter by a lousy sixty minutes? The only proven and acceptable benefit of Daylight Savings Time is that we get to eat an hour earlier. It really doesn't seem to do much to hasten the arrival of springtime.

When it comes down to it, maybe I'm as much a sun junkie as Myia. Someone should create a twelve-step program for that.

Hi, my name is Amy, and I'm a warmthoholic.

Unfortunately, it can be difficult, at times, to satisfy that precise infatuation in my specific locale. Pittsburgh simply isn't known as a land of tropical leisure, which is the primary reason I hold such a strong and lasting affection for Florida.

Yet, if cold temperatures must exist, I'd prefer we not overdo it. Anything below fifty degrees is simply unacceptable. I've just never appreciated that cool, tingly menthol feeling permeating my existence and invading my personal space.

I need an extra blanket just to watch the Disney movie *Frozen*. Let's revise the lyric: *The cold has always bothered me anyway.*

So, as you've probably figured out, I can't stand being cold.

I hate it, times two. Plus tax!

I would gladly trade the snowy white tundra of a Pittsburgh winter for the snow-white shoreline of Florida, any day.

Aside from the temperature here—or the lack of it at times—another problem is that I've never been very good at making snow angels. Mine always turned out as snow *blobs*, as if a skidding car had knocked over a fire hydrant.

In Florida, you don't have to worry about snow with prints of any kind. I do realize that the place isn't exactly the Promised Land or a kingdom flowing with milk and honey; the state does have a wealth of bugs, tropical storms, and waterspouts. It also contains an ever-growing population of sinkholes and pythons; one of which is capable of swallowing an entire house and the other its occupants. But from what I understand, Florida's summer boil eventually gives way to winter bliss, which is something I find quite alluring.

Though I don't know what my official designation would be if I could ever live there, it would probably be some sort of mismatched, hybrid, generic brand of beach bum and swimsuit model. Of most importance is that I'd be warm, year-round. I think I could handle that just fine.

No disrespect intended to the wonderful folks in Charlotte, but if I have to take a land voyage under treacherous winter conditions, I'd rather it haul me all the way to Miami.

What's another 700 miles or so?

3

Rubber and Ice

L ife can be funny, at times, how it often produces inexplicable anomalies, how it comes seasoned with questionable and quirky little nuances and those mystifying equations that just somehow end up making sense in their own peculiar way.

If these features make life amusing, mine is a hoot.

You see, like it or not, much like 3:00 a.m., winter happens. (If you didn't already know that, you can tell your friends you learned it from me.)

Until the poles flip or the purported global-warming assertion eradicates it altogether, cold weather will remain a stubborn nemesis and a personal adversary of one Miss Amy Brooks.

But I'm a big girl. I can deal with it.

Well…okay…at least I can deal with it.

The reason I'm able to accept winter's harsh reality is because I've found a pleasant diversion, comprised of the most basic elements that are vital to the existence of mankind in a hostile environment.

They are rubber and ice.

These are the essentials that are directly related to my sanity and survival during the dreaded winter months.

The way I see it, if temperatures must descend to the freezing point or negatively beyond, you might as well find good use for what it produces.

Fortunately, someone has done that; it's called ice hockey. This sport is a wonderfully resourceful invention and one of my biggest discoveries.

Sizing me up, one might suspect my favorite sport to be miniature golf, but it's actually Penguins hockey. I've almost come to appreciate winter because of it.

Hockey is the narrow icy corridor that carries me from autumn to springtime. You just can't find better entertainment than that which involves participants with clubs in their hands and knives on their feet, violently chasing a frozen disc of vulcanized rubber.

One thing I've discovered about watching from home is that it is crucial to wipe the television screen of those large black specks *before* the game begins. Otherwise, I'd find myself following the wrong puck.

As exciting as the game is on TV, nothing beats being there in person. I came to fully realize that in 2001 when my brother, Noah, and his wife, Theresa, took me to my first-ever game.

Our nephew, Cameron, went also. He was twelve at the time.

From then on, there was no turning back.

Before long, Cameron and I became a couple of season-ticket-holding, hockey-going fools. I always took my camera, and he snapped hundreds of great action shots for me.

Our second season in attendance, protective netting was added around the rink to prevent an errant puck from flying into the stands. Apparently, someone thought a fan might not appreciate taking one on the noggin while enjoying their nachos. It was also apparent that they didn't consider how that seemingly translucent mesh would affect my game photos. Though I finally owned a decent camera by then, its autofocus spotlighted the netting better than the players.

Are you serious?

That condition began a crazed fixation with me as I wanted to find the perfect camera and setting that would focus on the players from where we sat, instead of producing good, clear shots of a stupid, man made spider web.

As my official photographer, Cameron was equally affected by it, if not more so. He was the one who did all the work; I was just the boss lady.

Today, Cameron is a great photographer, though it isn't his actual profession. I can't help but to think that his photo skills are a direct result of our obsession for those perfect shots when we were younger. I'm sure much of his success derives from having had such a great "boss" back then.

Annoying nets and photos aside, I love ice hockey. And though I thoroughly hate the cold, I quickly fell in love with the frozen pond of what was then called The Civic Arena and, later, Mellon Arena. My passion for such a cold-weather sport has become the sweet paradox of winter, and I would eventually satisfy my craving for it in the new Consol Energy Center, across from where Mellon used to stand.

After about five seasons, Cameron was no longer able to accompany me to the games, due to an inconvenient and intrusive little thing called a job. Myia then took over as my official hockey buddy.

As much as I enjoy the game, I've always tried to exercise some self-control. I've cheered, celebrated, and ranted and raved to the fullest extent of the law. But I've also tempered it with just enough restraint to avoid being arrested.

Where would they place the handcuffs?

How would they fingerprint me?

It just wouldn't seem proper to put an esteemed civil servant through such a precarious ordeal.

Perhaps another reason I've never been stunned by a taser, blinded by pepper spray, or criminally charged is because I've learned to blend in with the rest of the natives; I now arrive at the games in style, wearing an official Winter Classic jersey of my all-time favorite player, team captain Sidney Crosby. The jersey was an awesome gift from my awesome friend, Eric. He's a Pens fan too.

If Eric were to ever move to Florida, I doubt that he'd shift his allegiance to the Tampa Bay Lightning. After God tased him with about a billion volts of it, I think he's had all the lightning he can stand for a while. If that's what it takes to keep him loyal to the Pens, then so be it.

You'll meet Eric in a little while.

As for the Pens, I believe I occupy the position of being their biggest and littlest fan, simultaneously. I just can't imagine a winter without them. That's why NHL lockouts are particularly distressing to me.

Eric insists that I'm an overtly optimistic person. Well, not when it comes to unplayed hockey games. I just don't like to be shorted. I'm already plenty short as it is.

Contrary to what some people might say, short fans don't appreciate short seasons because of contract disputes, or for any reason. Don't let them convince you otherwise. In fact, I prefer an extended season, with the Pens in the playoffs.

2010 was the first year that I decided to gain some facial hair when the Pens won their way into the postseason. This was before it was cool for girls to participate in "growing a playoff beard."

Of course, the idea is to wear it until your team loses. For me, the whole thing would involve a bit of imagination. My way of growing and maintaining a playoff beard was to get my picture taken with a beard and upload it as my profile picture on my social networking site. I'd then keep the picture up until the Pens lost.

Don't worry; it wasn't a real beard. My first one was made of paper, and I wasn't crazy about it not *looking* real, either. So, I pitched it and got some help from Mom with constructing a more authentic-looking replacement.

For that beard, Mom applied a layer of petroleum jelly and peat moss to my face. That did the trick. It looked much more realistic, and it became my official playoff beard.

I have to humbly admit, I do wear petroleum jelly and peat moss quite well. Not every woman can make it work for them.

Regardless of the outcome—win or lose—when the final whistle blows, it leaves me waiting the return of another hockey season, cold weather and all.

They say the Canadians invented the great game of ice hockey, but I'm not fully convinced; I think God created it as a consolation to those of us who have to endure the treacherous conditions of winter.

After all, the *Bible* says: *From the breath of God ice is made, and the expanse of the waters is frozen.* Job 37:10 (NASB)

So it turns out, winter was God's idea after all. It is actually breathed from His breath. But He has graciously offered us an alternative.

Hockey.

I suspect it's His way of saying, *Sorry.*

Apology accepted.

Now, freeze some water, drop the puck, and let's hit somebody!

Just one of the guys

4

Season's Greeting

O*n earth peace, goodwill toward men.**

Though some restrictions may apply—the parameters of which are listed below—I believe in that saying. I strongly desire those six words to become part of our world's existence, and I try hard to uphold my end of it by conducting myself accordingly.

What I find most appealing about this phrase is that it comes from the *Bible*, as part of what we typically call *The Christmas Story*.

With all of its traditions and trimmings and trappings, I thoroughly love all things Christmas, even if its arrival does confirm the start of another unwanted winter.

The way I see it, with the winter season being inescapable, there's no better way to greet it than with Christmas cheer. And it's okay with me if Old Man Winter greets Christmas with a onetime, sloppy, wet kiss.

But just a quick peck.

*Without penalty or consequence, the living application of this passage may be rightfully withheld from opposing forces and arch enemies of the National Hockey League's Pittsburgh Penguins. No exceptions, please.

In another of those strange and contradictory twists, I actually do prefer to have snow on that specific day. I'll even allow it on Christmas Eve, through the night, and into Christmas Day. But nothing more.

Is that asking too much?

I just won't go out and attempt to make snow angels in it.

Without challenge from any other holiday on the calendar, Christmas is, by far, my favorite.

It simply has no competition.

As the song says: *It's the hap-happiest season of all.*

Nothing compares to the elation and excitement it brings to so many, me included.

Christmas 2013 ranked for me as one of the greatest ever—in spite of it being part of one of the most brutal winters on record, with ridiculous negative temperatures and all-you-can-eat snowfalls.

If you've read my first book, you may recall how that, one year long ago, our home received a special package on December 24. Two packages, actually. It was the delivery of boy/girl infant twins in need of foster care.

Because of that book, I too received a special delivery on December 24, 2013. It was the book itself, the first physical proof copy of *Unseen Arms*, received from my publisher on the very day of Christmas Eve! This made my favorite holiday all the merrier. It was also fitting that the printer was located in the town of Bethlehem! (Pennsylvania)

Joy to the world!

Well, it added to my joy, anyhow. Christmas does that to me.

In what could otherwise be an entirely dismal time, winter has no choice but to officially arrive, smack-dab, in the midst of sparkling tinsel, twinkling lights, and glistening packages.

Best of all, it's empty, flavorless air suddenly becomes warmed and sweetened with the enticing aroma of Mom's handmade, home-baked, individually crafted, and perfectly constructed Christmas cookies. That's sort of her thing, her own personal trademark on a popular yuletide tradition.

And I do mean *personal.*

Every Christmas Mom makes an impressive spread of cookies. She takes a lot of pleasure in doing that, and she insists on making them without any help. She wouldn't permit me to lend a hand, even if I had one. There have been a few times when she did allow us kids to apply the sprinkles, but that's as far as it went.

Just being in the kitchen and watching her create those cookies makes it feel completely like Christmas, especially when she does the cutouts. While these aren't my absolute favorite to eat, they do represent Christmas in ways that are both decorative and delicious.

When it comes to taste testing and consumption, I've always been extremely partial to the Thumbprints, the Hershey kiss cookies, and the mouthwatering Ladylocks.

Among these assortments, the Ladylocks are the most tedious and time-consuming. So, Mom doesn't make as many of those as the others. Because of that, she would hide them in the basement so nobody would steal them. But those enticing cream-filled pastries were almost everyone's favorite.

Myia would always go down and sniff them out, no matter how well they were concealed, and she was sure to bring me one or two.

It was a victimless crime, right?

Along with all of this, I appreciate the enchanted sounds of Christmas carols and how they can be heard near and far. Whether bouncing with liveliness or wafting languorously, you can almost feel angelic creatures riding upon each note and measure. Among them, I prefer the classics, and I can't help but to sing along with pitch-perfect harmony.

Or maybe a little off-key. Whichever.

And let's not forget the mysterious cows that produce fresh eggnog. Christmas is the one time of year that they are finally siphoned for holiday ingestion. I love the stuff. Why wouldn't I? It's a symbol of Christmas in liquid form.

I also observe the age-old custom of sending and receiving Christmas cards, via post mail.

And then, of course, there's the shopping.

In upholding the canons of feminine law, I do like the hustle and bustle of Christmas shopping and selecting the perfect gift for the special someones on my list.

What makes this so fun is what we Brooks girls call our annual sister's day of Christmas shopping. That time and activity spent with Myia and Candy is priceless.

Throughout the holiday season and with all that it involves, what I enjoy most is giving. If I had to choose my absolute favorite part of Christmas it would be that, regardless of the amount of necessary effort.

When it comes to gift-wrapping, I'm kind of like Mom with her baking; I'd rather do it myself. For one thing, I love the smell of Scotch tape. Those of you with hands and fingers probably never get close enough to it to realize just how Christmassy it smells!

There have been a few times when the large gifts and the long rolls of wrapping paper have beaten me and I'd have to ask for assistance. But that's not to say I've never conquered them.

I remember one year wanting to be so independent about my gift-wrapping that I completely refused any help. I paid for that.

Where others break nails, I've often chipped teeth.

Four out of five dentists surveyed don't recommend that.

It's not that I run through the house with sharp objects in my mouth, but I do clench them in my teeth in order to use them effectively.

Fragmented incisors are an occasional result.

That year, instead of a hippopotamus, I came unnervingly close to wanting only my two front teeth for Christmas. While trying to cut wrapping paper with metal scissors, I added considerably to my chipped tooth collection.

It's not so bad though; I think of it as a hockey smile.

The other great ingredients of Christmas consist of laughter and crazy family memories that we've created with each good-ol'-fashioned holiday celebration.

The unfolding of one particular Brooks' family Christmas has become somewhat legendary. You may have already heard about it somewhere.

If you choose to continue following my story, please do so at your own risk. One thing you'll find to be true—even on Christmas—dumb never takes a holiday.

5

The Drunkard and the Pole Dancer

Before you become convinced that I'm from a strange, faraway land or a nearby uninhabitable planet, I must give honor where honor is due. Though Mom likes to take credit for my perfected foolishness, it's actually an entire Brooks family attribute.

It's common practice for us.

Standard procedure.

Our modus operandi.

If we were to form a country music group, we'd likely be called *Brooks & Dumb* because mine is a family that occupies the stage of the bizarre, and we never break character.

With us, what you see is what you get. So, you might be better off not looking sometimes. Each should come with his or her own product ingredients label, so the general public will know what we're made of.

With one element or another, my family is known to put the fun in dysfunction. The greatest evidence I can offer to support this claim is something that happened to make the most wonderful and most magical time of the year the most disturbing time ever.

But in an amusing way.

It was Christmas, and apparently someone had run a year-end special on a truckload of family dementia. Somehow, we ended up with the bulk of it that year; if not the entire shipment.

It began innocently enough, as many goofy occurrences and hilarious memories do. In fact, it was a casual but somber statement that initiated the whole thing.

There's something about the holiday season that often causes caring people to be more considerate of others who are less fortunate. That's a good thing. And Mom is one of those people. She cares year-round, but even more during the holidays.

While we were all enjoying the warmth and merriment of our festivities, Mom expressed her concern for a family suffering from alcohol abuse and other problems. She stated that her thoughts were with the children who had endured hardships and ill treatment, et cetera.

That's when my brother, Brian, injected his comment.

No one really knows what kind of thought waves were sloshing around inside his head that day. Maybe he was just trying to keep the mood light and cheerful. For whatever reason, as Mom was sympathizing for these hurting children, Brian blurted, "Oh, how well I know what that's like!"

"What do you mean?" someone asked.

Brian replied, "Well, you know how it was, with Dad being drunk all the time."

There it was. The pin had been pulled. The hand grenade had been lobbed. And no one threw their body on it to smother the blast, or did anything to neutralize the threat.

We could have at least done a duck-and-cover or some sort of tuck-and-roll maneuver—anything to prevent what would come next. But we didn't.

Instead, we all got caught up in the explosion.

From there, it was on.

Each became part and parcel to a whirlpool of weirdness and an all-out maelstrom of mania. The entire unfolding was a barrage of heavy arms fire.

"Friendly" fire, though.

Noah chimed in. "Yeah, we never knew what to expect when he was like that."

Another Brooks sibling piped up. "We didn't know if we'd get beaten or have enough food…"

And so it went.

I don't recall what the weather was like on that day or if there was any winter precipitation on the ground. But things were sure snowballing inside our living room with this bogus story playing out in Oscar-worthy performances.

Seeing us in action, you'd probably think that, if we all put our heads together, we might collectively equal about half a brain—with no frontal lobe development, whatsoever.

Someone blurted, "Well, you know why Dad drank so much, don't you? It's because Mom was always out pole dancing at the local clubs!"

"And it was so embarrassing when she'd be in the back yard practicing her routine at the clothes pole!"

"That's right! And Dad was always hollering at her from the upstairs window!"

It was wholesale hysteria.

Craziness on demand.

A true *Ripley's Believe It or Not* exhibit.

This ludicrous tale has managed to become a Brooks family holiday tradition. It's like a re-gifted fruitcake that keeps coming back. And as long as there's material, we keep adding to it.

The term "artificial intelligence" is quite suitable for our description. If we have any intelligence at all, it certainly isn't real. The worst part is that it's both hereditary and contagious.

So, I'm not the only nutcase in the family. The Pennsylvania squirrels love the whole lot of us. They stalk us, continuously.

It doesn't matter that I'm adopted; somehow it must have happened that I miraculously share my family's DNA and their malfunctioning chromosomes.

What contributes to this scene being so hysterical is that neither Mom nor Dad has *ever* been drunk. They have never even consumed an alcoholic beverage of any kind in their entire lives. Not ever!

As a creature named Shrek would say, "Really, really."

Maybe they aren't the Bailey's of 1946, as I stated in my first book; they are the Cleavers of 1957. This would seem more appropriate considering the Cleaver family was introduced to America in that year—exactly three months after my parents were married.

More fitting is that Rich and Janet Brooks are so sparkly clean that they squeak when they walk. Sometimes, they squeak when they're standing still.

Well, Dad does.

Sure, my family is a little nuts. This is well documented. It's especially true of Mom who holds her own framed certificate of nut-job authenticity. But you'll have to search far and wide to find morality and wholesomeness that beats or even equals that of my parents.

Yet, we've all branded Dad a horrible, falling-down drunkard, slurring and slobbering all over the place. Someone will probably up the charges and accuse him of wetting himself, indiscriminately.

And Mom is forever a pole dancer, even though she insists she's never stepped foot inside a dance club. Of that I'm not too certain, however. The intriguing and incriminating contents of an envelope suggests otherwise.

A woman handed it to Mom at church one day. Inside the envelope was a photograph of a pair of purple elbow-length silk gloves, taped to a pole. An accompanying note read, *I thought you might be able to use these in your act.*

I guess word gets around, you know?

6

Commendation

With the turn of the seasons and the passage of time—Christmas snow and summer warmth alike—life continues, as it has frequently been known to do.

All throughout, it has remained my firm belief that the state of Pennsylvania had never passed any active lemon laws when I was a child. Otherwise, my parents would have probable sent me back for having to persistently navigate the obstacles of muddled systems on my behalf.

When they took me home from the hospital, at eight days old, it was like a clearinghouse of limbless babies.

All sales were final.

No givebacks.

I came with a paper certificate and a plastic insurance card. That was as simple as things would ever be from then on for anyone who'd take me.

For those of you who think I'm handicapped, you are mistaken. But don't feel embarrassed about it. My parents had made the same assumption, and they'll be glad to know that they weren't the only ones to have once thought that about me.

It was firmly established that I was a Tetraphocomelia baby. Void of developed limbs, everyone could see my parts inventory was seriously lacking. But it didn't matter.

I was not considered handicapped, at least by the standards of one particular organization from which Mom had sought some assistance for me.

Though anyone who knows me would probably dispute it, I have always been deemed mentally fit. Therefore, I'm not handicapped. That was the word from the agency. That was the rendered verdict and their final answer.

It was their story, and they were sticking to it.

Apparently, I was going to be one of those who would fall through the cracks of a broken system. Or, maybe I was caught in the doughnut hole—that spot in the middle that doesn't exist.

Whatever the case, Mom argued with whoever would listen and with many who wouldn't. But their minds were made up; I wasn't handicapped. Maybe that's why my family never treated me as though I was.

In the frustration and impediment of it all, Mom finally asked, "What do I have to do, cut off her head?"

I'm not sure what their answer was or if they had even responded, but my head has remained attached for now.

Whenever I had need of something that my insurance was supposed to cover, such as a new wheelchair or passive arms to drive it, I was required to go for a checkup to make sure my condition hadn't changed.

After being measured and weighed and given a fifteen-point inspection—minus an oil change and free tire rotation—a medical conclusion was reached that my circumstances had not yet improved.

Sorry, doctors, no new limb growth this year.

Some of the ongoing conundrums faced by my parents were things pertaining to my wheelchair. And it wasn't because I simply wanted a replacement for one that was tricked out with the latest, most extravagant accessories or special-order luxury items. It was the basics that caused the biggest hassles.

First, the insurance company said I couldn't have a battery pack for my wheelchair. And then, they said I couldn't have a seatbelt.

What would I do with such indulgences, anyhow?

I supposed if I had someone push me all the time, duct tape and bungee cords might have held me in place, but those wouldn't have been favorable to the fabric of my clothing.

Who knows what they had in mind other than saving a few bucks? As it stood, there would be one chair, four wheels, no battery, no seatbelt, and several pitched bureaucratic battles.

Don't forget about the high impact encounter that we had with the drunken driver when I was five. That collision might have become an eventual bargaining chip as we had already discovered the importance of me having a proper seatbelt.

And who had ever heard of a powered wheelchair without the power source?

In all, it was a two-year struggle. When it was over, I finally got a wheelchair—with a battery pack *and* a seatbelt.

These are some of the things my parents had to wrestle on a regular basis. But life as we lived it was much too large and prevailing to revolve around someone as little as me. I was always glad about that.

The Brooks family stretched far beyond my own existence, abilities, and purported limitations, as there was always the continued supply of foster babies in need of love and practical care.

They came and went like little truckers at a weigh station.

It probably would have been best if Dad had just removed the front door from its hinges to allow them quicker and easier access.

Each was as a member of the family, regardless of how long they stayed or how quickly they moved on. As Mom mentioned in my first book, many of their stories were sad and disturbing, and most came with the organizational complexities that I did.

Against the mounds of documents, reams of paperwork, and bundles of pertinent records, Mom and Dad never determined exactly how many babies they had cared for during their fostering career. They lost track of the headcount when it was somewhere in the eighties. Luckily, I was able to help them pinpoint the precise number by using my very own foolproof system.

I painstakingly calculated the sum by using the highly sophisticated method of borrowing Sidney Crosby's jersey number. Thus, there were eighty-seven foster babies in all.

That should have earned them a combat medal.

Yet, regardless of the quantity, it was the quality of care that mattered most. I had experienced it firsthand. Remember, I started out as a foster kid before becoming a *real* kid.

Well, you know what I mean.

It didn't matter that I was initially a ward of the State; the care I received was topnotch. The same can be said of all the others who were fostered in our home—along with the Brooks family regulars as well. That was just how my parents have always done things.

And it eventually caught up to them.

For their selfless giving and their commitment to excellence—all alleged drinking and dancing aside—Pittsburgh's Children Youth And Family Services named Richard and Janet Brooks, *2002 Foster Parents of the Year.*

Unbeknownst to them, they had been nominated by a caseworker. Later, they were informed that they were officially being recognized with that distinction.

Of course, my parents wanted to downplay the whole thing. Though they did receive an art print and a certificate at an award ceremony held in honor of them and other CYF award recipients, Mom made it clear that she and Dad wanted to keep their part from the media and out of the newspaper. And they did appreciate that their request was granted.

They needed no fanfare, and they wanted no accolades.

Do you suppose they'd mind it being mentioned in a book?

Too late.

Z

Sour Arrow

Show of hands if you have them: how many of you have actually read my first book, straight up titled *Unseen Arms*? If you have, you likely remember the fundraiser.

Question: What happened to the arrow?

Remember that fundraising arrow, how it not only hit the target, but also passed through and—metaphorically and in reality—kept going?

Remember its figurative and literal sweetness from the untold number of chocolate bars that were sold to purchase my service dog and best friend, Jade?

Well, what happened to that arrow?

Where did it go?

As you think it over, you may want to put your arm down, so you don't look silly if you're reading in public.

But what happened to that arrow?

Granted, it's an imaginary one and the question is hypothetical, but where do you suppose it would have gone if that arrow were real?

May I offer a very tangible answer to a suppositious inquiry?

Somewhere along the way, that arrow became contaminated, and it came back to me, bitter and deadly.

That arrow—that sweet, precious, lucrative projectile—that spiraling dart of goodness and hope—somehow it returned as a poisonous spear.

Its target was Jade.

And then, it hit me.

The shot was fired late one night, beneath the cover of darkness. It was around my birthday time, late-September-ish, 2006. That was when Mom witnessed Jade having a seizure.

Though I was asleep and unaware of it, Mom sat with her throughout, to offer her comfort. A few weeks later, it happened again, and Jade became very weak.

I was devastated, but the veterinarian offered some hope. He put Jade on seizure medication, and it seemed to help for a while. I thought maybe she'd be okay after that.

On December 22, the entire Brooks family was wired for the sights, sounds, and celebrations of the holiday season. Having gathered at Myia and Mike's house, we enjoyed a typical festive evening in the form of another memorable Christmas party and probably added to the entertainment by teasing the drunkard and the pole dancer in our midst.

And all was well.

However, at night's end, we came home to find Jade lying at the back door, anxiously awaiting our return. Apparently, she had suffered another, more serious, seizure.

Her legs wouldn't work. She couldn't even move.

I didn't want to think about what was to come, but Mom tried to prepare me. Her prognosis was that Jade was unlikely to recover.

I wanted to give it the night, hoping for some sort of Christmas miracle. However, throughout the following hours of restless torment, I knew Mom was right.

In the morning, Jade was no better.

I didn't want her to suffer, so I decided to let her go.

I stayed holed up in my room until Dad and Noah carried Jade to the van.

Mom and Noah then drove off with her.

I never said goodbye.

Maybe that was selfish of me. Or, I might have thought that if I didn't see it happening, it wasn't really true. The one thing I was sure of was that it was the day before Christmas Eve, less than forty-eight hours before my favorite holiday. And while other homes were receiving packages and Christmas cards, I had been delivered a bundle of heartache.

Jade had been my closet friend. We shared a room together. I could tell her anything, and she'd always listen. But I couldn't bring myself to say one last thing. I didn't have the words to say goodbye. Nor did I attempt to find them.

I have often regretted that.

I could have nuzzled her a final time. I could have whispered my gratitude. I could have reminded her of how much she meant to me, of how much I loved her, of how beautiful she was. Perhaps I could have even managed a fake smile for her green eyes to behold before forever closing them.

But I didn't.

I did none of those things because it would have been too painful. I didn't allow Jade a final glimpse of me because I didn't want my last look at her to be one that beheld her sufferings. I wanted to erase those images from my mind and remember Jade for how she had been during the nine-and-a-half years that we were together.

What was she thinking in her final moments? Was she wondering where I was, why I wasn't there for her? Did her life and our time together flash before her eyes? Was her mind reliving fond memories of the two of us?

The vet told Mom that Jade had a brain tumor and that it was quickly spreading. He said I had made the right choice to put her down. But that didn't make it any easier.

Nothing about it seemed right.

By having to do that, I then became the target; the arrow of grief found me. And it pierced the core of my heart.

Not even the lights of Christmas would lift the darkness.

Penguin hockey couldn't distract the pain.

Later, when we were able to bring ourselves to talk about it, Mom recounted the final moments of Jade's life. As they were preparing Jade to be euthanized, she extended her paw to Mom like she'd do on the days when she felt sad about me going off to school without her.

Mom held Jade's paw.

And then, it was over.

She was gone.

Sour Arrow

You can bend it, break it, or whittle it down—only to find that it reduces to one simple word, the meaning of which I had never before experienced.

Sorrow

With Jade ~ always in my heart

8

Wisdom and Logic

J ade, my beautiful lady, was gone.

I missed her enormously, and I mourned her to exhaustion.

With her loss and the accompanying grief, I wanted to never again own another service dog. Having experienced the pain of her death—and at what was supposed to be the happiest time of the year—was something I was determined to not repeat.

I would simply do whatever necessary to avoid it.

Yet, before my tears had all fallen, Mom was on the telephone with the PAWS With A Cause organization, floating the idea of me getting a new dog.

When I learned that a trainer wanted to come visit me, I wasn't much in favor of it. I did reluctantly agree to meet with her, though.

Much of that meeting would consist of another evaluation of sorts, where I'd discuss the things that Jade was and wasn't able to do and what I'd expect of my next dog, should I ever decide I wanted one.

PAWS has an amazing policy: once you get a dog from them, you always have a dog from them, at no further cost. But I wasn't convinced that I should act on it. The persuasion wouldn't come until I met with Miss Penny who would be assigned as my trainer.

One thing that didn't feel right was the thought of trying to *replace* Jade, as if it would erase her from my life. But Mom and Miss Penny assured me that no dog could ever replace Jade and that I shouldn't view a new one as though it was there to do so.

Miss Penny was wise and crafty. She knew which of my buttons to push, and she knew how to push them. It was like she knew what I needed before I did. She was aware that I wasn't sold on getting another dog. So, when she came to do the evaluation, she brought Fawn along for the ride.

Fawn was a little black Lab and Miss Penny's personal demonstration dog. With tail happily wagging, Fawn came right over and loved on me.

It worked!

That was all it took.

The sale was made.

Miss Penny's experience, expertise, and wisdom had won out; I wanted a dog just like Fawn. From there, things escalated quickly. I soon received a follow-up call from PAWS with a breaking story: they had found the perfect dog for me.

It was a Poodle.

Wait…What? A Poodle? Seriously?

No offense to any poodles that might be reading this book, but that wasn't at all what I wanted. I had hoped for another Labrador, like Jade or like Fawn, but…a Poodle?

Not even a mix?

A *Labradoodle* perhaps?

I had lost a full-size sedan, and I'd be getting a subcompact in return?

A Poodle!

While wanting to be gracious, I just didn't know what to say.

Finally, laughter erupted on the other end of the line.

As it turned out, they really had found a perfect match for me. By PAWS standards, the dog was selected and trained in a very short period of time.

Apparently someone had placed a rush order on intelligent service creatures.

My dog, a female black Lab, was reported to have been one of the smartest and fastest learners to ever complete the PAWS training course. She was also delivered to me before she had reached the age of two. This is something that typically doesn't happen.

It was July when I got her, which means there was a turnaround time of only seven months. It all just seemed perfect and so meant-to-be.

Her eyes were a deep brown. She was totally black, nose included—unlike Jade who had a brown nose that matched her hair.

There was nothing funny looking about this dog, whatsoever. And there would be no finding her beauty on a second or third look; I could see it immediately.

Even the name, which she had come with, was one of uniqueness, sophistication, and dignity: Logic.

How appropriate!

I dubbed her "Lolly," and it fit her nicely.

When Miss Penny brought her in on that first day, Logic came to me while holding her own leash in her mouth. She pranced over and practically sat on my lap. Every now and then, she would tilt her head back for me to pet her.

She still does that.

During our at-home training with Miss Penny, we decided to assign Logic an additional task—opening and closing the trap door at the bottom of the stairs, which allowed my chairlift to stop flush to the floor at the base of the stairway.

In less than half an hour, she mastered it.

This is a job that I've now had her do multiple times a day. It allows me to come and go as I want without relying on a family member, house guest, or wandering intruder to perform trapdoor duties for me. That was a great bonus.

From early on, Logic could also pull my bedcovers without trampling me. Another bonus.

The covering process doesn't always go so well as the blanket often gets caught on my feet before reaching me. But my morning battle of the bedcovers had been effectually eliminated.

Thankfully, I would no longer have to perform my morning Harry Houdini straightjacket escapes. And there'd be no more squirming like Mom, who, years earlier, had to wiggle for all she was worth to free herself after stepping into the open hole when the trapdoor was left open.

In spite of my nighttime movements and undercover maneuverings—my relentless tossing and turning and twisting and tangling in my sleep—Logic is always able to uncover me with little effort. Even when I'm wrapped like a burrito.

Like Jade before her and like Bubba to Forrest Gump, Logic quickly became "my best good friend." She's my faithful sidekick. But let's be clear about that; though she is faithfully at my side, I have never kicked her.

Like me, Logic is a little short for her age, which is something else that makes us a perfect match. She is literally my little black shadow and the love of my life!

Not only is Canada credited with the invention of the great game of ice hockey; it is also the origin of Labrador retrievers.

Maybe there's a direct connection. It almost makes me want to forgive that country for sending their polar vortex conditions down our way, making the temperatures of January 2014 some of the coldest and harshest on record.

I'll get over that, eventually.

I can also get over the fact that Logic came from Michigan, near Red Wings territory. And it doesn't matter that she isn't covered with any wool; I'm convinced Logic is a dyed-in-the-wool Pens fan. She proved that two months after I got her.

In September 2007, while completing our final tasks with Miss Penny to gain our certification, we took Logic to a Pens pre-season game, in celebration of my birthday.

What a wonderful time we had, Logic included!

I'm thankful for Mom's intuition, I appreciate Miss Penny's wisdom, and I'm forever grateful for the bundle of Logic I received as a final result.

My days of mourning were ended!

Weeping may endure for a night, but joy comes in the morning.
Psalm 30:5 (NKJV)

Introduction

MEET MY FRIEND

U nder this heading, you are probably expecting me to turn my story over to Logic. After all, she is my friend, and she is right here in the van with us. Though she is quite an intelligent girl, I suspect I could easily lose you as my audience if I presented material from a Labrador retriever. Like the biblical account of Balaam's talking donkey, some may not relate well with it on a personal level.

While Logic has become and remains my dearest friend from the animal kingdom, Eric Fabian stands above most in the human realm. And he has prepared a little something for us to read on our way to Charlotte. Now might be a good time to pull it out.

For those of you who have hands and for those of you who know people, you can probably count on just one of those hands the number of close, exceptional, life-changing friends who have come into your life. These are God-sent, heaven-appointed, one-of-a-kind individuals. Nothing off-the-rack or run-of-the-mill; they are tailor made and custom fit for your life.

My family has always been the arms around me. They and others have sometimes been my hands and feet also. Eric is one of those others. He is part brother and part father-type, but always a friend, a true touchstone in my life.

Eric is made of the stuff the Village People sang about—a real-life "macho man." Yet, he's like an undercover Boy Scout, always looking out for his fellow man. Eric is a former federal agent and Harley-riding vice cop with a lot of knowhow and enthusiasm. He is highly educated and articulate. And he has a genuine concern for others, especially kids and the underprivileged.

Eric is like a living action figure. He's an avid outdoorsman. If it's out there, he'll get out and do it—hunting, hiking, camping, fishing.

He has also played recreational ice hockey and is experienced in martial arts. Of course, sometimes those two activities fit nicely together.

There seems to be nothing Eric won't try, including being struck by lightning. As a result, he is probably as much an alternative energy source as Myia. He naturally produces a sixty cycle hum if not properly grounded. I wouldn't be at all surprised if he has inadvertently sparked a few fires here and there.

Human electrical continuity aside, Eric is a doting father of four. Make that five if you count his motorcycle, and you should because he's been known to keep it parked in his family's living room during the winter months.

If I am the fifth child in the Brooks family, "Harley" is the fifth child in the Fabian home.

It seems God has not made nearly enough men like Eric. He's a different cut—only half a notch or so below "super hero." Yep, Eric has always been one of the good guys—a tattoo-wearing, heat-packing, tough-to-the-bone, good guy. Yet, as tough as he is, apparently I'm tougher. There was a day when I brought this tough cop to tears. I've asked him to tell you about it.

2

Tattoos, Tole and Tears

by Eric Fabian

The true, official, unedited title of this chapter is actually "*Tattoos, Tole and Tears and Other Preposterous Details.*" But Amy is a short girl, and she likes short titles. She seems to favor short chapters as well.

But before firing her manuscript in my direction, she didn't place any word count restrictions or any other writing limitations on me. In fact, she and Janet joked that mine would be the longest chapter of Amy's entire book.

While I am one of several who had encouraged Amy to share her story with the reading public, I had no thought that she might ask me to contribute to it. I'm honored by that. With reluctance, I agreed to a single chapter.

As for being expected to write the longest one, I have no desire to accommodate that. But with my obsession with details, I'm likely to do it, inadvertently. Please, accept my apologies in advance.

I am a person who is fanatical about details. A great portion of my fixation with them undoubtedly stems from my career in Federal undercover work and my current position as an investigator. But not entirely. I'm just wired that way, and I'm just weird that way.

It's the details between Amy and me—both delicate and rugged—that make our friendship all the more exceptional. At first glance, you likely wouldn't envision us sharing any commonalities. Side by side, she's a fresh-cut bouquet. I'm a desert cactus. She measures less than three feet in stature. I'm six-two. It is obvious Amy is a beautiful female, and I am totally not!

She is primped and proper and girlishly young. The sixteen-year age disparity between us makes her perpetual youthfulness all the more noticeable. And while she resides with her parents, I have been raising a family of my own.

These are a few of the perceptible details. However, it's the unseen ones, the specifics most folks are not aware of that have brought about mine and Amy's acquaintance.

That I would encounter the Brooks family isn't necessarily incomprehensible. Some would think it a no-brainer that we would all meet. At the time, we did attend the same church. But the details of my career and other decisions could have easily prevented our paths from crossing and our lives from pleasantly colliding as they have.

Like Amy, I'm Pittsburgh born and raised. I value education, and I value work. Both could have prevented me from ever meeting Amy.

My choice of college had taken me from Pittsburgh and from the church I had called home throughout my childhood. In that sense, it was a miracle that we met. Actually, it was a succession of miracles. Each came with their own fine print and with all of those intricate little things I so greatly admire: details.

Though I deeply loved my parents, my sisters, and my church, I left home upon graduating high school. At that time, I didn't know the Brooks family existed.

Desiring to attend a Christian college, I enrolled at Evangel University in Springfield, Missouri. There, I studied Psychology with the aim of utilizing it to help others.

Through a maze of unforeseen circumstances, immediately after graduation, I went to work for The Department of the Treasury, U.S. Customs Service. This placed me in a duty station in Charleston, South Carolina.

Five years later, I transferred to Arizona, to do narcotics work on the Tohono O'odum Indian Reservation. I was young and single at the time. I bought a beautiful home in Tucson. I was doing drug work. Life was great.

All the while, I had no idea if or when I'd return to my home town and to my home church. There were also no guarantees that I'd survive my career, giving me that as a future option.

During my assignment in Tucson, the Rodney King beating occurred in Los Angeles, which erupted into horrendous rioting there. With that, I was dispatched to south central L.A. to carry out nighttime four-man patrols in unmarked cruisers.

Among those California riots, Pittsburgh seemed to no longer exist. I was now in a whole new world that involved incredible violence and prevailing gunplay.

I suppose an inch is as good as a mile when you're missed by a potentially life ending bullet. In L.A., the shots fired around us might have fallen a mile away, but from that point on in my career, they began to hit closer.

One could have easily taken me out as a headshot, which was averted because I crouched at just the right second. Fortunately, I've never been hit, but it would have taken only one bullet to prevent me from returning to Pennsylvania alive. As a result, the Brooks family and I would have, obviously, never met.

After eight years as a Federal agent, I began exploring career opportunities back East—Pittsburgh preferably—so I could be near my family. In my research, I discovered Pennsylvania had an Office of the Attorney General, and they did narcotics work. When I called about it, a gentleman told me they had three positions open near Pittsburgh, but that three creditable candidates had already been tentatively selected to fill them.

"Look, what have you got to lose?" I said, "I'm coming back there next week for Thanksgiving. All I ask is that you just interview me."

The man fit me in for an interview, and he bumped me into the third hiring spot. I then moved back to Pennsylvania where I would do undercover narcotics work for the Attorney General's Office. This proved to be far more dangerous than working Federal cases in Arizona.

In Pittsburgh, I returned to my home church, Allison Park Assembly of God, after more than a ten-year absence. The church was generally a congregation of 1,800 people and had three services to accommodate them. It holds no comparison to a little country church where everyone knows each other.

When I returned there, I saw Amy and noticed she had no working arms or legs, but I didn't readily meet her or her family. They seemed lost amongst the crowd for a long time.

On the job, I drove the streets of old, familiar land that contained newfound hazards. I worked undercover doing street buys from armed teenage gang-bangers who would have no problem shooting me over a fifty-dollar rock; as compared to stopping a desert drug runner with a thousand pounds of marijuana who does not even run or resist.

It was while doing that work in Pittsburgh, where things hit the fan. That was when three of my fellow officers were shot during a drug deal—two of them with multiple gunshot wounds. And that was when I was forced to respond accordingly.

My parents had instilled a moral fortitude in me, which insists that you do not judge a man by the color of his skin, but by the character of his heart. I've always believed that, and I've always lived by it, then and now.

We all bleed the same color. On that day, I saw that to be truer than ever. I found myself soaked with blood; some from the bad guy, some from the good guys. White man, black man, criminal, cop, it doesn't matter. It's all human blood, it all runs red, and it all contains life.

Having been involved in a shooting, it was mandated by the department that I receive counseling. There were no restrictions placed on whom I could speak with as long as they were a certified counselor. It was under these conditions that I decided to call Dr. Marvin Jones, who was my favorite professor at Evangel.

He greeted me warmly on the telephone, and I quickly confided, "Dr. Jones, I shot a guy last night."

After a long period of silence, he asked, "Eric, are you in jail?"

Upon learning that I was a cop involved in a justified shooting in the line of duty, we talked about it for a long time. He then asked if I'd be interested in coming to Evangel to conduct a seminar on the topic of being a Christian in law enforcement. Hesitantly, I agreed.

It was eight months after the shooting when I returned to Springfield, Missouri, to give the presentation. At that point in my life, I was discontent with occasional, casual dating, especially since I had not found a good, compatible Christian woman, as I had hoped.

When I walked into the student union building, there was only one person in there because the contemporary Christian music group *Four Him* was playing in the chapel on campus. Everyone was at the concert except for this one person who happened to be reading by the fireplace. This person also happened to be a beautiful female.

After strolling over and initiating a conversation, I learned her name was Heidi, and she was a pastor's daughter from California. As a new student at Evangel, Heidi knew no one in all of Springfield except for the one person I was there to do a seminar for, Dr. Marvin Jones.

Heidi and I hit it off immediately, and we began cultivating a long-distance relationship. After four months, we were engaged to be married.

As for the shootings, everyone did eventually recover at various levels of recuperation.

When the drug dealer went to trial, which began about a year after the takedown, our taskforce team faced a courtroom full of hostile gang-bangers while our support from the Attorney General's office was practically nonexistent. This was greatly disheartening to me.

By the time the man was sentenced, it was three weeks before I was to be married to Heidi, and I began wondering why I was doing all this. I went home and called Heidi, who was back in California at the time.

I told her, "I think I'm gonna quit."

"Okay," she said. "What are you gonna do?"

I admitted that I had no idea, but I felt it was time to get out.

She said, "Go for it."

So, almost overnight, I went from *buying* grass to *cutting* grass. And then, after a short stint as a grounds keeper at a local golf course, I landed a job as the director of corporate security for an international company based in Pittsburgh.

Things at church continued as usual. From a distance, I saw the limbless girl in the wheelchair. I was curious what her story was, but I hadn't asked her. I hadn't even met her.

Many of us realize that God has an amazing, crazy, mysterious way of bringing good things out of bad situations. I can say by a stretch that I met Heidi because I had to shoot a man. That same stretch would conclude that I met Amy because our church was burglarized. The burglary actually occurred after a Sunday service and involved the theft of that week's offering.

When the local police were unable to solve the crime, I volunteered to work the case, and I was fortunate enough to solve it. Eventually, I formed a security team, which began working closely with the church greeters. Among the greeters were Janet and Amy Brooks, and that was how we finally met, midway through the year 2007.

I could tell Amy was an exceptional girl. Her smile and personality were so warm and kind that I couldn't help but to be drawn to her. She just has that effect on people.

Sometime later, while Amy was occupied with something, I pulled Janet aside. "I really don't want to be rude," I said, "but could you give me the backstory on Amy? Was she born like that?"

Janet gave me a brief rundown of Amy's history. As I learned more about Amy, I wanted to get to know her better as a friend, instead of as some distant consociate in a wheelchair. That was how our friendship began.

Eventually, I asked Amy why she didn't have working prosthetics. Her answer was very simple: they cost too much.

I then informed Janet that I would like to do what I could to help make Amy's life better, whether it would be raising money to help her buy working arms or whatever.

Janet was a bit guarded, even skeptical. She is a mother bear, and Amy is her cub. Countless others had come along previously offering to do this or that, and they never followed through. After a laundry list of those empty vows and worthless promises, Janet was leery of my proposal. She merely wanted to prevent Amy from getting hurt or from being disappointed.

This was all very understandable. I assured Janet that I couldn't predict or promise any particular outcome, but I offered a two-year commitment to help in any way possible. That was how *Arms Around Amy* came to inception. It was a startup concept to first raise awareness of this beautiful, inspiring girl, and then raise funds to help her get arms.

Ironically, the strongest opposition I ran into with that came from Amy herself. She didn't want the attention, and she didn't want people giving her money or doing things for her. If anything was going to be done on her behalf, she wanted it to be for others. She didn't want it to be about "Amy." Her selfless, humble attitude inspired me all the more, and the idea grew larger.

Amy's thought process was that there were others who were more in need. She insisted that, if there were donations to be made, someone else should receive it, not her. And where did she develop such thinking? She got it from her parents.

Rich and Janet invented altruist living. I suspect they hold a patent on kindness and humility. They perfected the art of compassion. Amy is just like them. Before I could become a mouthpiece to others, I first had to convince her and her family, which wasn't an easy task.

I felt it was just not acceptable for the healthcare system to say prosthetics were a cosmetic issue.

Are you kidding! They're called arms! We all need them!

Legs are a convenient commodity as well, but arms should be standard equipment for everyone, whether natural or prosthetic.

Apparently, functioning limbs are overrated for those who have them and for those who decide whether others should enjoy such luxuries as well. This just didn't set well with me.

If Amy would consent, if her family would allow, I would be a catalyst, become her arms and legs, to reach out and to step out on her behalf. But to honor Amy's request, it would not be exclusively about her; we would also establish *Arms Around Pittsburgh*.

My immediate goal with *Arms Around Amy* would be to assist Amy Brooks. The stretch goal with *Arms Around Pittsburgh* would be to assist others in the area who, like Amy, have physical deformities or disabilities. And so it is.

I'm privileged to have Amy as a friend. She is humble and thoughtful and gracious to a fault. In contrast, I would later come to know that, as sweet as she is, Amy does have a dark, evil side. Keep in mind, Amy has been known to be a redhead at times, and she can generate some fiery fury when necessary.

The only time you might see this is when her beloved Penguins have a really bad game. If you want to get on Amy's bad side, just get yourself on the team roster and go out and under-perform. If that happens, Amy Brooks will be taking names and checking numbers. And she will find a way to kick someone's butt. Other than that, you have nothing to worry about. At all other times, she makes Snow White look like a schoolyard bully because she is so ridiculously pleasant.

If you haven't picked up on it by now, Amy has a remarkable sense of humor and a warm, charming spirit. She may not occupy a lot of space on this planet, but I'm confident that she will leave a big mark on it. In spite of her vertical measurement, she is bigger than many six-footers I've met. Amy is a modern-day "David" who has slain the "Goliath" of disability, which has defeated so many.

Amy is a shining light, a positive influence, and an unbelievably inspiring person, who is going to owe me fifty bucks for writing such nice things about her.

Then again, maybe not because it's all true...except for the butt kicking reference; I just made that part up. And it isn't because she can't reach; she just has never been known for any unbefitting behavior.

What I find so amazing about Amy is her perpetual hope and optimism. While my light comes with a streak of stinging electricity, Amy is someone who can find a sunbeam in a nighttime thunderstorm.

With Amy, the glass is never half empty; it is always half full.

Some might complain, *It's well water.*

Amy would say, *Well, it's water.*

The topic of water is something that really caused me to see into the heart of Amy Brooks. It's a story that she has completely downplayed. But Janet shared it with me, and I would like to share it with you. Knowing Amy as I do, being the humble, unassuming person that she is, there's a good chance that she might ask me to delete it from my chapter. If so, I'll arm-wrestle her over that. If I win, it stays because I believe it's a story that should be written.

Janet told me that she was watching a television program presented by Life Outreach International, a ministry to which she and Rich had previously donated. Through this ministry, James and Betty Robison are highly active in world outreach crusades such as feeding impoverished children and other similar works.

On that night's program, the Robison's were promoting a safe water project for children in Africa. Amy came into the room and began watching also. Just as I believe everyone should have working limbs, Amy believes everyone should have clean, safe, drinkable water.

For a long time, Amy had been saving her birthday money and other miscellaneous scraps of cash to buy herself a television for her bedroom. She had saved up more than $700, but when she saw the need of those children, she was moved to action.

Having a particular compassion for children, Amy gave her entire savings to the project. And she did it anonymously.

It gripped my heart when Janet shared that with me, and I could have cried right then and there. Apparently, I was wearing my big-boy pants that day because I didn't cry. Almost, but not quite. I was able to man-up and suck it in.

Everything is fine, folks. Move along. The cop isn't crying.

Not yet. That came at another time.

My entire right arm is sleeved with tattoos. The sleeve is comprised of a series of symbolisms that represent my faith and various highlights of my life. Amy was admiring them one day, and she asked their meaning.

Each of my tattoos essentially tells a story. Among them is the lightning strike, which occurred while on a fishing trip in the Canadian wilderness. Six of us were hit that day. The others were among my very best friends—Mike Morse and his son, Willie, Tony Bruno and his son, Jonathan, and my son, Tanner, who was eight.

We had just returned to our tent to avoid an approaching storm, and we plopped down on our sleeping bags to wait it out. When the lightning struck the tent, Willie took the worst of it. From there, the shock passed through Mike and into me, and it reached ground through my feet. Tanner also felt it in his back.

Had it been a direct hit, we wouldn't have survived it. Instead, it appeared to be an offshoot of the actual lightning bolt. Later we found the entry point—a nickel-sized hole burnt through Willie's side of the tent.

We all recovered. Obviously, if the results had been different, I wouldn't have met Amy because of that. Aside from surviving and eventually meeting Amy, there was a particular benefit that came with the lightning strike: it was a pass to use it as an excuse with Heidi.

If you have the opportunity to experience a physical encounter with the business end of a lightning strike, you might find yourself becoming a bit short-circuited for a while. That was my experience.

Opposite my charred feet, I experienced a cognitive deficit that hindered me from recalling certain words. I could think of the word I wanted to say, but I couldn't say it. This anomaly only lasted a few months, and all of that went down in 2005. But if I would get into trouble with Heidi because I forgot something, I was quick to remind her, "You know I got struck by lightning, don't you?"

Amy seemed to appreciate my tattoos and the stories behind them, and she mentioned that she wished she could have some tattoos of her own. That was when the brilliance of my college education rushed to the forefront of my brain.

I went out and bought Amy a pair of tattoo sleeves—ones that are made of flesh tone fabric and printed with fake tattoos. We all had a good laugh when we slid one onto Amy's prosthetic arm, so we could get a photo together, showing off our tats.

At Christmastime of that year, Janet and Amy met me in the concourse at church. Amy was smiling as always, but brighter than usual. Janet handed me a gift from Amy.

When I opened the package, I found a boxed-frame photo of a Norman Rockwell painting. It was amazing. I had never seen anything like it in my life. Oh, sure, I recognized the picture; I had seen that many times. It was an image of a uniformed sailor in a tattoo parlor.

This sailor had a sleeve of his own, in the form of a long list of girl names running down the length of his arm. Each name had been crossed off, and a new girl's name was being added.

But there was something remarkably different and incredibly unique about this specific piece of work. This humorous, well-known photo was literally jumping out at me in three-dimensional form.

I was speechless, but I didn't realize that I had become deaf also. I didn't hear or comprehend when Janet said, "Amy made that for you."

I just stood there with my eyes popped out and my mouth hanging open. The details of the work were phenomenal. (Did I mention that I'm fanatical about details?)

After a long dumbfounded moment, I was finally able to form a mumbled sentence.

"Excuse me?" I said. "Where did you say you bought this?"

"We didn't buy it," Janet stated. "Amy made it for you."

The craftsmanship was flawless, the frame was perfect, and, oh yeah, Amy doesn't have any hands or arms! I tried to imagine the amount of time and effort invested in that picture to make it so perfect. And it was done for me!

They started to explain the project and how it was made. It was something called paper tole…Amy holds an X-Acto knife in her teeth… cuts out multiple images…glues the layers together with silicone…

I couldn't take it all in. And what I did take in I could not hold there. The emotions that churned inside me were indescribable. I couldn't help it—big-boy pants or not—I just had to cry. And so I did.

Of course, there's a good, logical explanation for all the gooey, gushy warmth I was experiencing: you know I got struck by lightning, don't you?

10

Artistic Boundaries

by Amy

MAKE A COP CRY!

Check!

I'm not sure how many thirty-two-inch females have reduced a six-two cop to a puddle of molten tears, but that's something I've now checked off my bucket list.

As for the fifty bucks I owe Eric for saying nice things about me, I guess I'd be getting off cheap if he holds me to that. Truth be told, I would've paid a hundred for him to *not* say those things.

To actually live up to Eric's words only makes my bucket list that much longer. It's a tall order to fill, and I'm standing rather short these days.

What was it he wrote, I make Snow White look like a schoolyard bully? Come on, I have nothing on Snow White. But I might give some of the Dwarfs a run for their money.

Dopey especially.

In reality, many personal upgrades are needed, which means God has a long bucket list of His own concerning His involvement and improvements in my life.

Not that He would ever kick any buckets; His is more of a to-do list, I suppose. And I'm sure it's quite lengthy if He's going to lead me where He wants me to be.

A lot of simmering needs to be done to boil out my imperfections. Sometimes a good tune-up is required. So, let's forget the Snow White association; Dopey works well for me, thank you.

As for my artwork, I'd venture to say most artists don't willingly set out to make people cry, cops in particular. Artists typically intend their creations to inspire or bring pleasure. Some aim to provoke thought and discussion. Others dazzle with amazement and wonder or emanate peaceful reflection.

Art often displays clever elegance and ingenious ambition that extends far beyond the normal reach and abilities of many intelligent but inartistic persons. It has also been known to reveal egos and eccentricities.

Many works are steeped with charm and humor. Certain pieces have been known to deliver a message or tell an entire story. Art can instill awe and conjecture. It can be rich with emotion and wit. Some pieces have even caused great controversy.

But as far as I know, art seldom produces tears.

I guess that's another personal niche of mine.

Every artist has them—their own flair, their individual brand, their signature style. That's what sets them apart. It's what makes them favorites.

Of the artists I most admire, three are at the top of my list: Bob Ross, Thomas Kinkade, and Charles Fazzino.

A vibrant painter with an ordinary name and trademark afro, Bob Ross is best remembered by many in the art world as the creator and television host of *The Joy of Painting*, which aired for many years in the United States and Canada.

Ross was an inhabitant of the great and magical land of Orlando, Florida—a warm weather guy, I'd imagine. He had never seen a snowy mountain or a snowy anything until he enlisted in the Air Force and was transported to Eielson Air Force Base, which, ironically, is located in nearly the very center of Alaska.

How's that for artist contrast?

The scenery there inspired Ross and fueled his artistic brilliance. As a result, snow-covered mountains and wintry landscapes became the predominant subject of his work.

That's the type of cold weather image I can appreciate.

Keep it confined to a picture frame where it belongs.

Emitting from the frames of Thomas Kinkade's work is glowing light. That was his genre. Light was his forte. He was so incredibly good at it that he is forever trademarked the "painter of light."

His work has made the world a brighter place. Though we lost his light when he passed, his paintings continue to illuminate the lives of those who are fortunate enough to own them.

For reasons that are unfathomable to me, Kinkade was considered "controversial." His paintings were often labeled as "mall art." This notion is far beyond my comprehension. Quite possibly the insults he endured was a rejection of the "light" that his work promoted.

Regardless of what the critics had to say of him, before his death, Thomas Kinkade was reported to be America's most-collected living artist. There's not much to condemn about that.

I've never been a fan of abstract art, including my orange and blue award-winning monkey that I wrote about in *Unseen Arms*. That's why I admire the works of Ross and Kinkade. Their themes are immaculately detailed and realistic in form. The picturesque bucolic scenes they created will undoubtedly live on for generations to come.

Paintings are not the only forms of art that I appreciate. I like variety. I admire all displays of creativity—drawings, design, decor, architecture, crafts, et cetera.

I applaud such abilities.

Well, inwardly I do.

I particularly like Charles Fazzino for his works in three-dimensional paper tole (pronounced: tool), which of course is very similar to mine, but on a larger scale.

Charles is also a master at silkscreen art and has successfully achieved and perfected a three-dimensionality technique with his silkscreen serigraphs. His creations are amazing.

I can only wish to be so gifted.

In time, I hope to stretch myself to his talent level. If that occurs, I might possibly come to physically measure a bit taller by an inch or so.

Or maybe not.

With sharing the same passion for works in paper tole, Charles Fazzino once offered to feature me in his blog, which is quite an honor. That could be something we'll work on in the future. He has also graciously invited me to visit his gallery displays in New York, and I'd love to take him up on it someday.

One comparison Eric didn't make between himself and me is that Eric travels all over for work and for recreation, while the bulk of my existence has generally been found inside the measurements of our home and within the margins of my bedroom.

Eric lives life in the fast lane. I've pretty much lived mine in a subcompact parking space. But that's fine. The important thing is to live a life that is motivated and moving in a positive direction.

Art helps me to do that.

Though I'm usually quite close to the ground, art helps keep me grounded. It presents a clear focal point that lies beyond my own contiguity.

Because of art, I remain occupied in ways that are constant and constructive. I also find it to be more honorable than trying to print my own money or hack into government websites.

Art allows me to be an observer as well as a contributor. I spend a lot of time comparing my work and talent to that of other artists, and I'm continually amazed by their creativity and ingeniousness. I often wonder how they come up with their ideas and how they are able to bring those concepts to life in their work.

I feel that my art differs in this area. If I'm lucky enough to get a good idea, it almost never comes out the way I envision it. Then again, the end result could be a specialized form of art unto itself, whether by intent or by accident. And who's to say if other artists don't experience the same insecurities?

We only see their finished product and never really know if what they created is actually what they fully envisioned. Nor do we know if they had to throw it away and start over a few times before getting it right.

Regardless of the outcome of my efforts—my alleged talent or lack of it—I do believe that what I'm able to do is a God-given ability. I couldn't do it without His strength and guidance. Having this awareness, I want my work to honor God and encourage others by demonstrating the concept that we can truly accomplish difficult tasks and attain challenging goals, in spite of our circumstances.

Still, my artwork is not perfect. One contributing factor is that I simply have not invested enough time into developing new and better methods.

As limited as I am, there are two additional artists that I must acknowledge for inspiring me to cultivate the skills that I do have. These artists are females, and they are so completely unknown that even they don't realize that they are artists.

They are my sisters.

As stated in *Unseen Arms*, I credit Myia for initially exposing me to the world of arts and crafts. Though I was told I displayed that interest as far back as preschool, my first real memory of anything artsy was admiring Myia as she painted little light-up plaster Christmas houses.

Naturally, I wanted to paint with her, but I couldn't quite maneuver and conquer those pieces at the time. So, I opted to paint the flat ornaments instead.

Those lay on the table offering little resistance and voicing no complaints as I approached them, face first, with a sticky paintbrush clamped between my teeth. I'd like to say that that was my jumpstart into artwork, but it wasn't much of a jump; it was more of a slow crawl until I got better at it.

Myia and I also had fun decorating our own tee shirts with puff paint. First, we applied iron-on transfers of cartoonlike images, and then we decorated them however we saw fit. We also made a couple of Christmas sweatshirts.

With the puff paint, there was no daubing of colors or stirring with a brush; I simply squeezed the contents from the tube with sheer jaw power and created some interesting, one-of-a-kind patterns.

The hysterical part is that we actually wore those shirts.

Though I might deserve it much more than Thomas Kinkade, I hope no one criticizes my lapse in style and my lack of judgment back then. I was only about nine. But you can think whatever you'd like about Myia; she was much older.

Either way, I'm sure the fashion critics can appreciate that we never attempted to introduce a Brooks line of ladies' custom outerwear.

At school, like every student, I often doodled on the covers of my textbooks. That was back when we used brown grocery bags to make throwaway slipcovers for them.

My scribbling and squiggling brought me to the swift realization that I didn't really have much elegance for drawing. Nor did I have a lot of patience for it. The best I could do was replicate cartoon pictures—mainly Disney and Nickelodeon characters.

For someone with a growing passion for quality artwork, I eventually became disgusted that I couldn't create better drawings than that.

As I got older, I chose to give more attention to painting and decided to tackle the very ceramic houses that I had watched Myia paint. By then, they weren't as difficult. They did put up more of a fight than the flat ornaments, but after conquering them, I was able to sell some of those little houses and other painted sculptures. With that and the discovery of paper tole, I eventually abstained from drawing altogether.

Candy influenced me artistically by introducing me to some of her little friends. Well, they aren't friends in the literal sense. They're actually dolls, but they look quite real.

We made them from a kit, by taking a sculpt of baby parts made of silicone and coated with heat-set paints, layer upon layer, heating and reheating them in the oven as we went.

It's called "reborning." We didn't make that up. It isn't Greek, and it doesn't derive from Mom's "hillwilliam" terminology. The process is reborning because the products are known as Reborn dolls.

Apparently, someone thought that label might contain better market appeal than saying the babies are "oven-baked."

Candy and I worked as a two-person team on them. I realize that's sort of how most babies are produced anyhow, but that's not what I'm talking about. In making these creations, I did the paint mixing and most of the applying while Candy assembled the baby and rooted the head with mohair.

Reborn dolls look and feel like real babies. They are unquestionably much nicer looking than the shirts I made with Myia. (Sorry, sista.)

The little things are so lifelike that you expect to see them stir and fuss at any moment. Their limbs certainly look more realistic than my prosthetic arms.

Candy and I haven't made any of these dolls in several years, but if we decide to take it up again, I might sneak an attempt at making some of those parts in my size.

While produced primarily for collecting and display, there are some parents who buy Reborn dolls as play dolls for their kids. However, that wasn't something we recommended when we sold them. And there were some adults who treated these dolls like actual living babies.

Also not recommended.

Eventually, my adoptive art partners, Candy and Myia, moved on to other interests. Though I remained dedicated to art, I too have moved on— determined to enlarge my creative limitations, regardless of my challenges or restricted office space.

My physical work area consists of a four-foot-round table in my bedroom, which is where I do most of my artwork and other intricacies. My computer desk is a countertop that extends about five feet along my wall. Both of these furnishings are lowered, which allows me to work from a comfortable height.

For me, art has become a lasting journey that has transported me into an incredible world. It's a voyage that I continue to experience. It's a lifestyle that I thoroughly enjoy. From where I stand, from where I sleep, from where I work—little by little, inch by inch—my borders are steadily expanding. I can only pray that yours are also.

Whatever your passion—whatever your calling, whatever talents you possess, whatever dreams you dream or gifts you have—may we all come to realize that our only true limitations are the ones we place on ourselves.

It really doesn't matter if my artwork is favorably comparable to others as long as I stick with it. The same can be said of your interests and goals as well.

According to Greek philosopher Aristotle, "Passion for the project brings perfection to the work."

If we truly have that passion and act on it, maybe your accomplishments and mine are a little closer to perfect than we think.

WARNING: Do NOT try this at home

11

Occupational Hazards

These are reportedly the last words of the late, great artist Leonardo da Vinci: "I have offended God and mankind because my work didn't reach the quality it should have."

Even though he was knocking on the doors of eternity, he must have been joking, right? How could da Vinci's opinion of his work be that it lacked quality enough to be offensive? Had he lost his passion for it?

How could Thomas Kinkade be openly criticized and his paintings publicly insulted? Was it an attack on him as a person?

Clearly these men were among the best of the art world.

Where would my work stand in comparison? In da Vinci terms, how greatly have I offended? By Kinkade's experience, to what degree would my work be condemned?

These were accomplished artists amidst a wide population of incredible talent. I'm a small fish in a small pond, with limited resources—certainly not a da Vinci or a Ross, Kinkade, or Fazzino.

Still, art is the one thing that I've always wanted to do with my life. I'd like to have studied it formally, but I didn't for the same reason Mom chose not to pursue a nursing degree; tuition cost was the primary factor.

Also, body exertion was a chief contributor for me. When I graduated from high school, I closed the book on the idea of continued education because it was so time-consuming and physically demanding.

Not that I'm antisocial or anything, but the best-case scenario for me would be to enroll in online classes and work from home. This would save time, eliminate transportation hassles, and reduce physical strain.

I do regret not being formally educated in the field that I love. I'm hoping it could still happen someday, though I do realize art is a difficult study and a tough profession.

Over the years, I've learned just how hard it is to become successful at it, and I now understand why there is a segment of artists who are known to be "starving."

Doing the work is hard, selling the work is harder.

Selling original artwork is simply not as easy as falling off a log or, in my case, down a flight of stairs. But I have put my artwork into circulation a little to make it more accessible. I've managed to sell some at shows here and there, but mostly online. To showcase my work, I set up a website called *WaddlesWorks,* which is now incorporated into the AmyBrooks.org website.

The name is self-evident.

From *Unseen Arms* and for notes to add to your file of useless knowledge:

Amy was born with seal limbs

Amy used to have duck feet

Amy waddles like a penguin when she walks

This is all an aquatic theme that I've had working for me, and I decided to use it when naming my website. However, I only drew upon the penguin portion of it.

Combining my longtime admiration for the Pittsburgh Penguins and my present-day waddling like a real one, *Waddles* is me. *Works* is my art.

My displays mostly consist of three-dimensional works in paper tole. However, I also posted the Reborn dolls that Candy and I made. Most of them are several years old now, but they haven't aged any; they have completely managed to remain in the infant stage and just as lifelike as ever.

Additionally, I decided to add a few of my paintings to the site. Somewhat by force, I have also uploaded a couple of drawings because Eric prodded me to do them.

It seemed if anyone was going to challenge me to break free of my comfort zone, it was Eric. He nudged me from the realm of familiarity, beyond that which was more simplistic.

The nerve of him, right?

Maybe it was payback for making him cry.

But don't worry yourself about Eric; the tear-shedding episode hasn't really been all that traumatic for him. His line of work has prepared him to handle all sorts of unpleasant situations. I'm sure his police training included a class on surviving emotional distresses induced my limbless female artists.

As far as unpleasant situations go, I have completed a few in-home tutorials on those as well. They weren't necessarily pass/fail courses or schoolings on which I was graded toward an Honors award; they were more the subject of annoyance and lessons in endurance.

Though I have found a sliver of definitive coziness that encompasses my surroundings, and though I have discovered security that accompanies my minuscule boundaries, there are also many hazards and discomfitures associated with them.

These remain in full existence, regardless of my borders or restrictions because they are a small portion of who I am, and they are an element of what I do.

First is that which Mr. da Vinci battled—the idea of your work not being suitable for visual consumption. What's worse is to think that the end result is actually offensive to God and mankind.

I have to say that I've never been so critical of my artwork to consider it offensive. This may prove that my abilities are not equal to those of da Vinci. I'm pleased with some of my finished products, with others not so much.

So, I think I can relate somewhat to da Vinci's anguish.

On some projects, I feel like I scored a hat-trick. On others, it seems I fanned every shot. Disgust and disappointment sometimes accompany the pieces that don't turn out as well as I'd like.

Even so, the words of French writer Voltaire stand as a helpful reminder: "Don't let the perfect be the enemy of the good."

Through it all, I continue working at art because art is my work. Essentially, I find it to be a two-cycle component with about a fifty-to-one ratio. I mix fifty parts recreation to one-part vocation, and most of it seems to turn out okay.

There are other things that I've mixed as well.

Note to self:

Always put hair in ponytail before working with Elmer's glue, with no hands

I learned that lesson the hard way, and it took more than one self-imposed seminar to really get it. On one occasion, I glued my hair while making a project with Popsicle sticks. Another time was while working with paper tole.

Obviously, I'm not the brightest crayon in the woodshed.

As for the vocational side of my art, I do sell my work, but I make a lot more pieces than I actually sell. I'd offer them all for free if I could. I'd love to just give it all away with no questions asked and no strings attached. Giving them, sharing them, handing them out—I find that to be much more fun and rewarding than accepting people's hard-earned cash for them.

However, famine is not a risk that I wish to add to my collection of artistic dangers. If I dispense of every piece without charge, I'd surely be signing my name to that long imaginary list of starving artists.

Of course, I'm only kidding about that. I have encountered several hazards and endured my share of aches and discomfort, but hunger pangs have never been among them. You'd think it should be, though. You'd also think I should have built some immunity to physical pain by now.

In art sales, I barely earn enough to cover the monetary costs of creating it. If this were my true source of income, I would have died years ago.

For example: 2012 was quite a busy year for me with art projects, in terms of work for the entire calendar year. As I sold them, I kept all the money from each piece in an envelope along with the receipts for my art supplies.

When I counted up the cash, I found that I had accumulated $836. Not a huge haul of loot, obviously, but for me it was substantial. After I subtracted the money spent, my profit was a whopping $54.71.

My busiest year ever and all I made was fifty-four bucks!

An artist maybe, but a businesswoman I ain't!

Apparently, I had become a no-profit organization, without even trying to. Yet, my bills are paid. And I've never gone hungry.

Though I'm quite fuel-efficient and don't usually have a large appetite, I do eat well without selling much art. I also eat well with blistered lips caused by producing art.

You see, sometimes even my successful works can afflict various forms of suffering. It all goes back to watching Myia do arts and crafts when I was really young. In addition to the little light-up houses and ornaments, I also remember her making Christmas wreaths.

In the process, she used a hot glue gun to attach the decorations. Maybe kids shouldn't be eyewitnesses to such things, but I was very attentive.

Years later, I desperately applied that observation.

Or attempted to.

I don't remember exactly how old I was or what I was trying to make, but I was young and absolutely *needed* a hot glue gun because no other glue would hold. (I knew to avoid Super Glue, even if it would work for the project, because the last thing I wanted was to adhere my lips together and physically become a starving artist.)

In my demand for hot glue, no one was available to help me at the time, which wouldn't have mattered anyhow; I didn't want any help.

Most likely, Mom was unaware of what I was about to do. I can't imagine her allowing me to take on a hot glue gun without permission and qualified assistance. But the task was going quite well, thank you.

No arc flashes or electrical shocks.

Hadn't caught my hair on fire.

Didn't glue my face to the table.

More importantly, I remember the art project was coming along nicely, too. That is until those little strings of glue got in the way. At that point, my efforts became an exercise in stupidity.

But at least I was getting some exercise.

If you are eating dinner while reading this, you may want to set your plate aside for a moment; this next part might present itself as a viable appetite suppressant.

When attempting to remove the strands with my mouth, I accidentally touched both the upper and lower regions of my lips on the gun's smoldering metal nodule.

With my lips sufficiently TIG welded, I practically became a fire-breathing dragon. The result of my carelessness was a three-alarm lip fire and second-degree burns that created large blisters. My parents weren't too thrilled about that.

Then again, neither was I.

Pain and unsightliness battled one another to claim the greater position on my mouth. Between the two, I think it was a tie.

And as if the timing couldn't have been any worse, the incident happened just a day or two before we were to set out on another trip to Delaware for me to do some more prosthesis sampling. Unfortunately, they weren't able to fit me for a pair of prosthetic lips.

Where's a Mrs. Potato Head kit when you need one?

One thing's for sure; the whole experience depleted any interest I might have had in becoming a flaming sword juggler. Other than that, I don't remember the burns stopping me from doing anything. It certainly didn't hinder my eating skills.

No way. Not this girl.

If my lips could talk, they'd tell you.

Pain or not, deliver me a pizza and watch what happens; I'll guarantee consumption in fifteen minutes or it's free!

In March 2013, Sidney Crosby took a puck to the mouth on a slap shot from fellow Penguin, Brooks Orpik.

Nice name, but a bad aim, apparently.

With multiple teeth flying in various directions, our star player went down in an instant. From there, he underwent extensive dental surgery, which put him off the ice for more than a month.

Crosby's biggest comeback problem was an inability to chew and eat well. He should have called me; I could have helped him with that.

Hockey players take pucks to the teeth. Carpenters smash their thumbs with hammers. It's all part of their occupation. And then there's me.

When I'm trying to be careful of something, I basically tuck my lips in, so whatever I'm grabbing doesn't actually go inside my mouth. This being the case, the burns were more above and beneath my lips, but they were genuinely scorched, nonetheless.

The scabs lingered for a few weeks before they finally healed. But I really didn't care much about how I looked at that point. It was just another battle wound. From there, I eventually went on to graduate from burns to cuts.

It seems I'm no one-trick pony. Not only have I proven my lip burning abilities, I've also discovered other ways to endanger my health through artwork.

Paper tole is my favorite expression of art. As it turns out, working with tole is both a reason for strain and a relief of stress.

Because of the techniques I have to use and the prolonged periods in which I'm subjected to my working positions, 3-D art is physically demanding on my neck, back, and shoulders. This creates a lot of muscle strain and skeletal fatigue.

Conversely, this work is very much a mental stress reliever. It is serene and calming and helps melt away many concerns of life. Bringing these pieces together and watching them develop is extremely satisfying for me.

So, sometimes art is a pain in the neck. Sometimes it's a joy to the heart. I find the unfolding of those circumstances to be pretty much equally divided.

Of the type of X-Acto knife that I use to cut the paper tole, my choices are restricted to the plastic handled variety because they are less harmful to my teeth.

However, my teeth are not necessarily less harmful to them. The handles become gnawed and bent after a while and have to be replaced. While they are much cheaper than replacing teeth, the plastic handled units are becoming increasingly difficult to find.

Unlike a pen or pencil, I can only hold the knife in my teeth for the necessary grip, firm cutting support, and accuracy. This is also more conducive to personal safety, but sometimes things don't go as they should.

Though my teeth encounter fewer hazards with this particular cutting tool, my other parts remain at risk. Softer handles or not—no matter how you slice it—the blades all cut the same, human flesh especially.

No need to become alarmed; I've never been a night stalker or the slasher type. My hacking has all been self-directed.

I'm also not what you'd call a cutter. Not intentionally anyhow. Sometimes I just happen to slice or jab myself when using an X-Acto knife.

Over the years, I've probably experienced more knife wounds than your average street brawler. Some have left nice gouges and a few scars, but nothing yet requiring stitches, staples, or reconstructive surgery.

To join those particular nicks and gashes, I'm forever getting paper cuts on my lips and arms. I have also acquired them on the tip of my nose, but don't ask how I'm able to accomplish that. I'm just not sure.

Maybe it's because I had an early start at developing the necessary skills to potentially hurt myself, such as displaying my downward stair-falling ability when I was very young.

Injuries or not, I love art. I'm dedicated to it in spite of the risks. Assorted cuts and burns have basically become part of my job description as a hands-free, self-styled artist.

Yet, I've wondered why Dad won't loan me the use of his power tools. Safety first, stupidity last, I suppose. But the way I see it, those priorities should be permitted to switch places as circumstances call for it.

Shouldn't they?

12

The Cactus of Pittsburgh

Based on his word choices, it seems Eric and I are in a campaign. One metaphorical illustration he presented was that I am a "fresh-cut bouquet" and he is a "desert cactus."

Continuing as editor-in-chief and self-appointed critic of his chapter, I must admit that I'm not completely sure of his meaning—other than to merely spotlight our dissimilarities, in which case his juxtaposition is blatantly incorrect.

Eric is always on the go and at full speed, possibly due to the electrical overload in his system. There are days when my body's potentiometer is dialed down to near zero, and I move at a snail's pace or slower. That's the best assessment I can offer.

He claims to be a cactus?

I'm a bouquet?

Please!

I'm sure he meant it as some sort of compliment, but those are practically fighting words. Well, maybe political jargon at least. If so, that would make him my opponent, despite being one of my dearest friends.

The bouquet? Make like a bride and toss it. Pour out the water. Put away the vase. It really doesn't represent me well.

Thus, my run for office is official. But don't worry; I won't allow things to become too ugly. My first promise to the American people is to keep the political attack ads and the administrative mudslinging to a minimum.

My fellow citizens, I can assure you that I am not a fresh-cut bouquet. I wouldn't say Eric is either. I'm not at all suggesting that he is the flowery type. But if it helps me to secure your vote, you can believe that if you wish.

Either way, he's no cactus. Sure, he gets a little bristly when he hasn't cuddled with his razor in a while, but that's about as far as it goes.

Though I'm no expert on them, I do know Pittsburgh isn't celebrated much for its stickly, prickly cactus development. In fact, you wouldn't think there'd be a single one of these arid stubs growing anywhere near this part of the country, but there is. There's only one. And contrary to what my opponent says, I can rightly lay claim to its title.

Please, allow me to explain my position, and you'll be convinced to cast your vote for me on this important issue.

Unlike Mom and her lonely potted palm tree that she's always had standing in our living room, I've never planted a cactus. I didn't grow one or draw one or cut any from tole. I've never painted a cactus, never made one from ceramic, never constructed one of paper mâché.

My friends, I *am* the cactus.

I became one, initially and officially, in the latter part of 2011. That was when my cactus activity began, due to being laid up for about the entire summer.

My single biggest challenge and most painful activity was trying to walk in the way that I've been accustomed. I'm not talking about hiking the Appalachian Trail or backpacking across Europe; I simply was unable to get around the house as needed.

Other than sunbathing with Myia, I couldn't do much of anything because of relentless, increasing pain in my left hip. Of the two, that is my worst side. I often refer to it as my "bad leg." The biggest problem is a constant pinching sensation, which I've had there since our literal "run-in" with the drunken driver.

Because of that, I've undergone a sequence of lifelong chiropractic adjustments to help alleviate some of the pain and pressure in my hips, back, neck, and shoulders, which is pretty much all of me. Throw in a shampoo and they would have had me fully covered.

In addition to my mismatched hip sockets and crash injuries, my back is a bit irregular as well; my spine is straight instead of having a natural curve as it should.

These physical conditions have caused me numerous problems. It seems there was never really a point in my life when I was not in some degree of pain because of them.

For me, an aching hip or a sore back carries the potential of causing a complete body shutdown. These problem areas could place me on life's sidelines where I am downgraded from active participant and relegated to casual observer.

That is very exasperating. So, more often than not, I just push through the pain and keep going.

At times, it seems everything except my hair hurts. And even that bothers me by getting in the way a lot. But I can live with the inconvenience. It is the body strains and pinched nerves that become my primary dilemma.

Over time, my birth diagnosis and the car crash had come together in a collision of their own, bringing me an assortment of aches and a measure of impedance.

Chiropractic care has often worked wonders for me by dismissing those symptoms, but there were also phases when nothing helped. That has been my typical situation since as long as I can remember.

In 2011, something changed. Everything intensified for me. That was when my hip attacked me like a starving carnivorous beast. When attempting to walk, the pain was unbearable. It was also unfamiliar, a new brand of hurting that was different from the pinching condition. It didn't replace the pinching; it was coupled with it.

Added to the bodily discomfort was my elevated level of aggravation from simply being unable to freely move about. When I did walk, it required extra time and a lot of energy and painful endurance to get from point A to point B and back again.

As the condition worsened and it became more difficult for me to get around, I worried that I'd degenerate to a point of never walking again. My worry was that I'd go full circle and have to resort to the use of a walker similar to what I had as a kid.

I soon paid a visit to my trusty chiropractor, Dr. Brian Green. He and his staff have helped me wonderfully over the years and have always been there for me anytime I need them.

Because of me, they might be considering a name change to *Pine Valley Chiropractic and Book Store*. Aside from relieving my pains and discomforts, when *Unseen Arms* was published, Miss Mary, at the reception desk, took it upon herself to start selling my books from her workstation. And she has sold many of them, one after another.

But my appointments there were never for literary purposes.

They were always about pain relief.

The official medical finding of this newly formed pain, in 2011, was that I had a deep muscle strain and inflammation. That and my normal abnormalities met and mingled into a perfect storm of physical torment. Only time and rest would heal it. Other than that, there was not much that could be done.

To ease the pressure and reduce the chance of further injury, Dr. Green advised me to stay in bed for two weeks.

After half that time, I couldn't tolerate the immobility. I hated not being able to do anything. Besides, it wasn't helping. I wasn't improving.

With no disrespect to Dr. Green, I knew I couldn't continue to follow his recommendation of total bed rest. I had to go over his head, to the very "Top" if necessary.

From my experience, you just can't go any higher than God.

In every service at our church, the congregation prays as a whole for those who need it. The following Sunday they prayed for me.

As Creator, God has a myriad of wondrous methods and inventive ideas when it comes to answering prayer and helping our circumstances.

After the church service, a friend came up and suggested that I try acupuncture therapy. He then provided the phone number of the guy his son used for relief from a sports injury a couple of weeks prior.

One thing I hate more than being cold is being in pain. So, I was willing to try it.

The first part of the process was to see if my insurance coverage would include these procedures. It didn't. Apparently, the pain in my hip was going to soon spread to my pocket as well. But something had to be done. I'd just have to bite the bullet and pony-up the cost.

As usual, Mom took care of scheduling my appointment.

If you might have dozed off along the way, or if you simply haven't realized it by now, nothing with me is ever standard or commonplace.

It comes from a seven-syllable Greek word, which wouldn't have been worth mentioning by name to the acupuncture therapist because it's something no one has ever heard of before, right? Instead, Mom would merely ask to speak to him on the phone to offer a quick heads-up on what he'd be dealing with concerning me. Without using any fancy terminology or giving a lengthy explanation, Mom would simply tell him that his new patient would be a young female who was born without arms or legs.

Short and simple, just like me.

Our church friend had given us the office number of a male acupuncturist, so Mom assumed that she'd get a man on the phone. She got Miss Sydnie instead—Sydnie Bryant, L. Ac.

I cannot imagine her level of astonishment when Mom told her that she'd be treating a person who was born without limbs, but she truly was shocked by it.

However, it was not because she had never heard of such a condition; it was because she had! It is called congenital Tetraphocomelia, and she had become familiarized with it many years prior.

With that, it would be our turn to be shocked, not once, but three times. A trio of surprises, a hat-trick of astonishments, soon greeted us.

Of course, our first surprise was to learn that Miss Sydnie was familiar with the terms of my birth condition. Thankfully, she was willing to bring me on as a new patient in spite of it.

Meeting Miss Sydnie, I found her to be very kind and soft spoken as if she was aware of my shyness toward new people. She also seemed to read my unspoken apprehension about being stuck with a bunch of needles. We joked about how small I am, paralleled to me being a big baby when it comes to pain. Her pleasantness helped me to relax and made me feel relatively comfortable, considering the circumstances of our meeting.

We then got down to business.

Thus began my exposure and my experience with the realm of cactushood of which my opponent, Eric, has none.

The session ended an hour later, and surprise number two came along like a swinging door that smacked our fannies as we left: there was no payment due! Miss Sydnie had voluntarily offered to treat me without charge!

Obviously, we were grateful. It wasn't anything we had anticipated, and we had no idea why she would extend such a shocking offer. She said she just wanted to see me get better.

We wouldn't discover the full reason for her generosity until my second visit. In the meantime, I had some healing to do.

Though the treatment itself wasn't painful, the aftereffects were. Being confined to my hip, I could refer to them as "side" effects. I might also say the acupuncture treatment really "stuck" with me, but those would be corny jokes. So, I won't say those things.

Besides, it really was no laughing matter because I could do nothing but lie in misery for an entire week.

On my second visit, Miss Sydnie was upset to learn that I had suffered for that additional amount of time. And it was completely unacceptable that I hadn't called her about it and returned earlier so she could tend to it right away.

Initially, Miss Sydnie had applied the needle sticks directly to my hip region, which seemed reasonable to her at the time. But I've always played by my own rules; what may have normally worked well with other patients didn't work for me.

As was the case for the ER doctor who examined me after the car crash, I wasn't the typical patient or what you'd call a "normal case." With me having fewer pressure points, shorter nerve paths, and less…everything, Miss Sydnie didn't really have much to work with.

Be it a little or a lot, our human parts are all connected. Sometimes the root cause or optimal treatment area is not located where the pain is actually felt. Therefore, she would have to try a different approach.

On that second visit, Miss Sydnie took another stab at it.

A series of pokes, actually.

Instead of concentrating her efforts directly on my bad leg, she focused on other areas of my body and completely ignored my hip region.

By doing that, I noticed an immediate improvement.

Soon after, I was hit with that third surprise from Miss Sydnie: before she was born, her mother had given birth to a baby boy who was born with full-scale Tetraphocomelia.

He didn't survive past birth.

This has always been a source of anguish for Miss Sydnie. Additionally, the question was never answered as to whether the baby was actually stillborn or if the hospital staff simply allowed him to die.

Precise cause aside, he was an older brother who never existed, due to the same birth condition as mine. This was the reason Miss Sydnie chose to treat me at her own expense.

After that second visit, I continued to feel a little better with each weekly treatment.

Miss Sydnie did good work. Though I valued her skills and appreciated her generosity, when I recovered, I was hoping my cactus time was completely fulfilled. Unfortunately, those hopes were dashed a year later when I encountered a sequel to the hip problem.

The hurting began as a moving target—back aches, neck pains, the usual at first. It then settled into my rib area, the same immobilizing pain as with my hip, but further north.

The pain soon intensified and lingered for a week.

Finally, I went to Dr. Green for an adjustment. This only left me feeling worse. He adjusted me again a few days later, but I was still hurting.

As it turned out, it was no wonder the chiropractic tune-up didn't help; a person just can't fire on all cylinders when they have a piston sticking out. Well, that might be how Dad would describe it. Dr. Green would tell it a little differently.

The real problem was that I had somehow managed to dislocate a rib. It just sort of popped out of place. The painful result of that strange occurrence was a lot of pulling and tearing at important parts in the surrounding area, such as muscles, and tendons, and Amy guts.

It came in excruciating fashion.

Dr. Green seemed to realign everything alright. I guess he returned the rib to its proper cage and securely padlocked the gate to prevent any future escapes.

Like setting a broken bone, it had to be done.

But no one said I had to like it.

The rib had been out of place and roaming free for over a week. The inflammation from that misalignment and the movements to relocate it caused me a greater level of misery. After a few days and a second adjustment, I was no better, and there was nothing more Dr. Green could do to help the situation.

Act one, scene two. Same song, second verse.

Or whatever.

My sleeplessness and tormenting discomfort led me back to a personal reunion with Miss Sydnie. The result equaled more cactus time to add to my résumé.

As before, my treatments were a week apart and greatly needed because of the constant agony. When venturing out in my wheel chair, the weight of my prosthetic arms made the pain worse.

I remember being in church one Sunday during that time. As the service went on, I could feel my entire left side drooping and pulling away from my body. I had no strength to correct my posture and little stamina to endure the pain.

As I underwent further acupuncture treatments, Logic offered comforting companionship. She also provided physical relief. The pressure of her snuggling against me alleviated some of my bodily strain, which helped lessen my suffering.

During my time with Miss Sydnie, I have accumulated hundreds of needle sticks. My opponent, my challenger, my rival has zero.

Ladies and gentleman, Eric is no cactus.

Think about it: have you ever known a cactus to get hit by lightning? More than anything, that would make him a personified strobe light.

In conclusion, and as I make my run for office, I believe I have shown that I truly offer a more convincing cactus rendering than Eric. Should it ever appear on a ballot at some time, you'll have to cast a vote for Amy Brooks on this one.

For those of you who might be leaning the other way, needle sticks from tattoos don't count.

His are drawn on with a crayon, anyhow.

Probably by his kids.

Thank you for your support!

13

Into the Hornet's Nest

Well, here we are! We have finally arrived! Dad is a real pro, isn't he? Retired, but a professional, nonetheless. He has maintained his stellar driving record, and after a nine-hour journey, we have arrived.

And you are nearly halfway through my second book!

I hope the ride has been good for you and for those who are leisurely reading along from the warmth of their living room or from the comfort of their toilet seat.

As for us Brooks travelers, it appeared that my inner 3:00 a.m. concerns had come true. Not everything went well or according to plan. It has been a rough one for us.

After an hour of running around like a chicken with its limbs cut off, I finally rolled into the van. It would only be my parents and Logic and me...and those of you who rode along within these printed pages.

Noah was supposed to come also, to absorb some of the wheel time. He was up, willing and ready to go, prepared to take the first turn of the helm. Literally, a last-minute deterrent prevented him from joining us. With that adjustment made and a travel prayer said, we began our expedition without him.

But wait! Where was Logic? Why was she not hopping in?

It turned out that she was confused and nervous.

We had opted on renting a van instead of driving our own, figuring we'd be covered if there were any mechanical issues along the way. Should anything happen we could get a replacement and continue on without much delay and devoid of sticker shock for unexpected service work.

But Logic never read the rental agreement or the van's operator's manual. She didn't know what was going on or why things were different. Though considered a "handicapped" vehicle, this van was designed much differently than ours, and she wasn't even sure how to climb aboard.

In our van, Logic doesn't use the ramp; we keep it folded until she hops inside. But the rental has a ramp that comes down automatically when the door opens. We figured out that it disturbed Logic to have to walk on it.

With the other side door having no ramp, we would have to let her enter and exit there, so she wouldn't stress over that. But there were other things that couldn't be countered so easily.

Our van has carpet flooring where Logic seems to have good static cling or some natural doggie Velcro condition, which allows her to ride along comfortably.

No slips, slides, thrills, or spills.

The floor of the rental is just plain sheet metal, allowing for easy cleanups. With nearly every turn of the steering wheel or press of the accelerator or brake pedal, the blanket that Logic was lying on became a magic carpet ride. That was very upsetting for her. She was very skittish of being so…skid-ish.

Every time we'd stop for a bathroom break or for food or fuel, we'd try to straighten out her blanket. But it never lasted long. At one point, I contrived the brilliant idea of parking my wheels on the edge of the blanket, hoping it would hold it in place.

The idea turned out to not be so brilliant because it didn't work. She continued to sled and slide all over the place, thus becoming an unintended "sled dog." It hurt my heart to see her in such distress. And I was already in enough pain as it was.

Obviously, the rental was fully designed for a wheelchair passenger, which is a description that I've worn throughout my lifetime. But like Ground Hog's Day, even the van came with a glitch. It isn't an electrical problem or a mechanical malfunction; it's a design flaw that might be best described as over engineering.

My ride location contains an additional, extra-large, very heavy shoulder belt that was made to stretch completely around a wheelchair. It's the same kind that was in some of the school buses that I had ridden as a kid. But the driver usually didn't make me wear it. Or if they did, it just wrapped around the seat, not across my chest like a standard harness for a regular seated passenger.

It's bad enough that my body isn't used to being in my chair for a long period of time without it taking its toll. That belt made it unbearable. It was more like a conveyer belt than a shoulder harness.

I really didn't want to wear it across my body, but this was a time when Dad wouldn't listen to me. He refused to give in to that which he thought would compromise my safety. Hence, he required me to drape the burdensome shackle over my chest, instead of just across the chair.

When sitting, I typically lean forward to avoid direct pressure on my tailbone, but the safety belt didn't allow me to do that. The thing was so tight, with absolutely no give, and it pushed me hard into my seat in a way that I don't normally sit. This prolonged riding position created overall soreness and low back pain.

In addition to the heavy belt, what made the trip most intolerable for me was when my phone was on low battery. As we drove along, Mom left her seat to plug in my charger. Servicing this need greatly contributed to my physical suffering.

Of course, it was no walk in the park for Mom, either. She had to tiptoe her way over a sled dog, luggage, and everything but the kitchen sink to reach the charging port located toward the back of the van. But seeing there were no open trap doors to fall through, she made it back just fine, and Dad continued motoring down the highway.

With my phone plugged in behind me and on the opposite side of the van, I had to turn in that direction the best I could and was forced to elevate my shoulder. This allowed me to balance the phone to prevent it from being pulled away by the cord.

All the while, I kept up with my GPS monitoring, lip texting, and social media postings in that awkward and strenuous position.

Having done that for hours, my back and neck and shoulder didn't appreciate those particular activities with me riding like that. And they let me know it in no uncertain terms.

In spite of my aches and pains, this actually seemed to be the best way to get me to Charlotte.

Planning a trip for me is rather complicated. Carrying out those plans can be eventful. There is a lot involved with arranging such an outing because I can't just hop on a plane and go with ease or elegance. We discovered that when we flew to Disney World after my freshman year of high school.

As part of the proposal for me to make this speaking appearance, I had been offered roundtrip airfare, which I greatly appreciated. However, I would also need my parents and a van to get around. Plus, I wanted to take Logic along. It seemed better to just get a rental in Pittsburgh and drive all the way.

An additional inconvenience that we encountered came in the form of a missing breakfast ingredient. A major ingredient—Cracker Barrel.

Unless you were born into or adopted by the Brooks family, or unless you have physically vacationed with us, you probably wouldn't have expected to stop at Cracker Barrel sometime along the way. For those of us who are regulars, eating there was something that was supposed to have happened.

Whenever we vacation or take a significant road trip, we always seek out a Cracker Barrel for a good "hearty and home style" breakfast or lunch. It's actually our favorite place to eat when we travel.

In so doing, I can only hope that I'm not the only patron who has eaten Cracker Barrel's thick white sawmill gravy by the spoonful, thinking it was mashed potatoes.

All gravy aside, having not taken a real vacation since 2005, we were looking forward to enjoying breakfast there and visiting the little country store. To help facilitate the idea, I had become a Cracker Barrel stalker, downloading an app to my phone that provides the location of every Cracker Barrel restaurant on Earth and in its surrounding galaxy.

If you ever want to know where they are, just ask me. Otherwise, that intuitive and helpful information will go to waste because we didn't use any of it.

In the weeks leading up to this jaunt, I spent valuable time Mapquesting every destination that we'd hit. I printed and organized each of them into a handy, easy-accessible file for Dad to have in front of him. The only thing I didn't do was laminate them or place them in a shadowbox frame.

Dad was already familiar with the routes and exits to North Carolina, but he likes to have something more tangible to reference. I figured he'd need them to find the hotel and other precise locations, anyhow.

Being all over it as I was, I also informed him that I had Google Maps on my phone. At first, none of that mattered to an old-school trucker. He insisted on using the mass-produced, professionally printed, store-bought, fold-up maps.

Who uses those things these days? And why do they never fold back up like they're supposed to?

Ironically, when Dad decided, later on, to give my phone app a try, the battery was drained from all the texts and social media messages that I was getting from family and friends, sending me their love and support and votes of confidence. So, it was back to the old "misfolded" fold-up maps. As for the ones I printed, he didn't use them, even once. He also didn't stop at a single Cracker Barrel because we weren't able to fit it in.

While you were reading—several miles back and a few chapters ago—we pulled into a rest area, so Dad could lie down and relax for a bit.

There is an old English idiomatic term that references the concept of taking a short nap—Forty winks. That's what he needed.

To prevent falling too far behind schedule, my vote would have been for thirty-nine, but he probably could have used at least fifty. And he deserved it. So, I was willing to negotiate.

As it turned out, Dad's interpretation of forty winks translated into a forty-five-minute nap, which delayed us by at least that much. For a quick breakfast alternative, we chose a McDonald's drive-thru. From there we continued to drive-thru, including driving-thru lunchtime. What was great, however, was that we also did a drive-thru of the Blue Ridge Mountain region.

At first, I thought I was seeing things.

The Blue Ridge Mountains really are blue in appearance.

But don't confuse them with Kentucky bluegrass, which is actually green for some odd reason.

As for the mountains, I didn't know anything about these majestic formations when I first saw them. Their beauty drew me in and rendered me speechless. Staring in silence, I observed how beautiful they were and how blue they looked—as if God had taken a big-ol' Crayola to them.

If they weren't colored by crayon, I wondered what made them look that way. Was it the sun beginning to peek out from behind the grey rain clouds? Or something else? Maybe it was my imagination.

Just then, Dad pointed out that we were "entering the Blue Ridge Mountains."

Ha! I wasn't seeing things!

To quote actor Jim Carrey, "Alrighty then!"

So, we continued driving-thru, without me fearing that I was hallucinating or seeing mirages of blue-colored landscape. And we drove right on "thru" to our destination. And here we are!

The Cactus of Pittsburgh has safely entered The Hornet's Nest! Welcome to Mecklenburg County, North Carolina.

The Queen City of the Old State.

Land of the Tar Heels.

Home of the Bobcats.

NASCAR country.

Downtown Charlotte!

Though it rained most of the way—sometimes heavily—I'm pleased to see the weather is clear, and the air temperature is much warmer. How's that for a little southern hospitality and a favorable first impression?

It is just after 1:00 p.m., and the sun is beaming brightly.

As much as I'm beginning to dread the idea of giving a public speech, I'm glad to have arrived so I can be freed of my restraint.

If you're wondering why we're here exactly, it's the direct result of *Unseen Arms* being published. Because of that, I've been invited to the Ignite Justice Conference. I am actually scheduled as one of the keynote speakers.

Yikes! What were they thinking?

And what was I thinking to agree?

But I did. I showed up. So, let's get it done.

Not so fast for you, though. I don't speak until tomorrow, anyhow. Tonight we'll just connect with the rest of our posse, set up my book-signing table, wander into some of the conference presentations, and meander about the place.

I don't mean to be rude, but if it's all the same, I'd rather not invite you inside. You see, I've never done an appearance like this before—not at this level, so far from home, or in front of so many people. And the one I did before was a long time ago.

I guess you can say this is my first rodeo.

And I just don't know how it will all turn out.

So, I was thinking you could wait here in the van.

It won't be that bad; Dad does it all the time. Whenever he takes me somewhere, he usually doesn't want to come inside or drive back and forth. So, he just waits in the van, selflessly and patiently—sometimes for hours. You can do that, right?

Besides, we don't know what this place is like. If there are any hockey fans here, I'm sure their allegiance belongs to the Hurricanes in nearby Raleigh. We might have to keep our guard up.

Though the place looks friendly enough, I'm gonna have to do a full recon of the area to make sure that it's safe. There is quite a storied history here, dating back to the American Revolutionary War.

In his failure to conquer this city, Lord Lieutenant and Commander-in-Chief Charles Cornwallis called Charlotte, "a hornet's nest of rebellion."

Apparently, it was a fitting assessment because that rebellion and its resistance sent him on high retreat with his tail between his legs. I know I've said it before, but again it seems appropriate: *Sorry, Charlie.*

But sorry or not, he escaped with his life, and the name stuck: "The Hornet's Nest City."

We hate leaving you behind like this, but you should be fine. You'll never even know we're gone, especially Dad since he doesn't say much.

The keys are in the ignition if you need to run the heater or if you want to listen to the radio. You can also help yourself to whatever snacks you can dig up.

Feel free to catch some fresh air.

Enjoy a cool walk.

Take a seventh inning stretch.

Scratch a halftime itch.

Or, it might be best to just settle in, sit back, and relax. You won't have to look too long or search very far to find plenty of reading material to help you pass the time.

Part Two

Moving On

There are far, far better things ahead than any we leave behind.

~C.S. Lewis

14

Stage Fright

At countdown to zero and the moment of impact, it was the single most stressful, most terrifying decision of my life. With my heart frantically beating the air out of my lungs and my skin crawling with cold perspiration, my entire body mimicked a sweaty palm stuffed nervously inside the metaphorical glove of a motorized wheelchair.

My head was whirling. My thoughts were spinning. And my stomach was on the verge of heaving as the time approached for me to speak on that day—convinced that I didn't really belong there.

What am I doing?

Who am I kidding?

What am I trying to prove?

A beloved *Bible* passage says: *Surely goodness and mercy shall follow me all the days of my life.* Psalm 23:6 (KJV)

But where was the fulfillment of that promise at that specific time? Where were those particular benefits? It seemed they had fallen off somewhere or had become lost someplace behind me. How did I find myself being escorted by panic and dread? Where was Mr. Goodness or his partner, Mr. Mercy?

Missing in action, apparently.

Did they take the day off? Had they called in sick?

Were they spending some unused vacation time?

Maybe I was the one who had gone astray. Perhaps I had outrun them. Could I have taken a wrong turn somewhere?

Facing the unavoidable reality of speaking before a live audience, I was literally becoming ill with fright and could have fainted at any moment. To offer the less appealing, unladylike, unedited description of the event, it was the closest I had ever come to hurling my guts out without actually doing so.

I felt like a fish out of water.

Or, more like a penguin in a sweltering desert.

Why did I agree to this?

Am I seriously going to throw up?

Obviously, I was in the wrong place. I was sure of that. But there was no turning back. No escape hatch to drop into or magic box where I could disappear.

I had to go through with it because neither fainting nor vomiting were especially appealing options. Besides, I had given my word. I said I would do it. So, I pushed ahead.

My speech was written out meticulously, and I pretty much just read it, word for word—trembling, line by line. Scarcely did I even peek at the audience.

The presentation was about fifteen minutes of sheer terror before an audience of only two to three dozen people, several of whom were my family and some distant friends. Somehow I survived it without requiring a medical evacuation.

Thankfully, I had avoided the loss of consciousness and the display of projectile vomit. But it was a horrendous experience, regardless.

Those are my clearest perceptions, my honest rendering of events on that day, early in the year 2006.

Up to that point, I had grown in my faith. I was more mature as a Christian. And though I typically don't believe in making New Year resolutions, I had begun that year with one.

My intent was to become a brighter light, to be actively affective, to make a positive difference. I was resolute to being a useful vessel, a helpful tool, an instrument of righteousness that would honor God and benefit others. So, I began 2006 by asking God to use me in whatever capacity that He saw fit.

Without hesitation, He took me up on my offer. But it wasn't in a way that I would have expected or desired. Who wants to be chucked into a fiery furnace, right?

Evidently, that's what God thought I needed. Being asked to share my story in a public speech was equivalent to that.

The request had come from a friend who insisted that I share my testimony at this small church, just a short drive from our house. For some reason, I agreed.

I have to admit the outcome was tenfold better than I could have ever predicted—aside from not passing outward or throwing upward.

Even so, I knew I never wanted to do it again.

Not ever.

One and done.

That's it!

I wasn't a public speaker, a preacher girl, or a televangelist. I was just me, Amy—a quiet, stay-at-home, keep-to-myself artist person who might be a better witness for Jesus by just minding her own business.

But the audience didn't seem to think so. It turned out that goodness and mercy were hiding amongst them. Their response was very warm and accepting. They were all so gracious and supportive, which was very encouraging to me.

Their kindness likely aided in my trauma recovery.

Still, the trauma was unforgettable. It scared me half to death! And it was that trauma—the complete distress and duress of it all—that I so easily remembered after agreeing to speak in Charlotte in 2014.

That's why I didn't reserve a spot for you.

That's why I didn't invite you inside, live and in person.

The worry of more trauma was the reason I left you waiting in the van.

Though eight years had passed since I had done my first speech, the fear remained in my memory. Of course, it would be best to remember the love of the people, instead. I could draw from it and from the many prayers that were with me.

I had to keep my eyes open and my vision clear—looking for hints and signs that I was doing the right thing. I would need something to propel me forward and give me added strength to fulfill my commitment.

What I wanted in Charlotte was a shot of inspiration, a dose of encouragement, maybe a key to lock up my worries or open a door of confidence. I would have to find some external help, some outside influence, something beyond myself.

Otherwise, I wouldn't have anything meaningful to say.

15

The Key to Inspiration

O ccasionally with some and consistently with others, we, as humans, are known to search for answers and seek purpose. We look for hope and meaning, long for justice, crave fairness, and expect equality. Often, we pursue the trails of solitude and wish for peace at every turn and tranquility with each rise and fall that appears before us.

With a passing familiarity or a headstrong assurance, we have sought that which is spiritual or embraced the sensational. Hesitant or scared, some dabble and sample, merely dipping their toes into the churning tide of surrealism.

According to English poet Alexander Pope, others, as fools, "rush in where angels fear to tread."

Many among us are known to watch for signs along the pathway of life, desiring to catch a glimpse of confirmation or a hint of true direction.

Most likely, we will eventually see what we are seeking. By way of search or by keen, intentional observation, we will find what we are looking for. Often, it is divine inspiration or simple encouragement in one form or another.

This is not an excessive wish or too much to prayerfully request. To find such a treasure is enchanting. But to have had it *find me* is practically incomprehensible. I discovered this to be wondrously true in Charlotte.

As countless other droplets of grace have been known to do, the sweetness of inspiration had searched for me and had found me. Or, perhaps it had been simply awaiting my arrival. Whatever the case, it was an unexpected blessing, nonetheless.

And it came through nontraditional means.

Granted, I didn't arrive as a seasoned traveler. But I'd never seen it before. Haven't even heard of anything like it. There it was, regardless, in its undeniable, unbelievable form.

I knew perfectly well that it was a room key, though unconventional from keys as we typically know them. This kind resembles a credit card in size, shape, and appearance—thin plastic with a magnetic strip, likely measuring 2-1/8 by 3-3/8 inches.

It was a key to a hotel room. More specifically, it was *the* key to *our* hotel room, and it carried a message that appeared to be written to me alone.

That flimsy plastic card, that room key in disguise, contained these printed words: "**Stay Inspired**."

Are you kidding me?

Again, as with the Blue Ridge Mountains, I had to wonder if I was seeing things. Again, thankfully, I wasn't.

One might do well to discover such an inscription inside a fortune cookie at their favorite Chinese restaurant, or we might envision it printed on a church bulletin. But who would expect to find such encouragement stamped on their hotel key in a far-off city to which they had traveled to offer an inspirational speech?

For me, it bore the same significance as being written by the finger of God on a tablet of stone. More than a room key, it was a sign, a memo from my heavenly Father that everything would be alright.

Yes, I was inspired.

And I intended to remain so!

16

Ground Support and Ocean Sounds

The stratum of support that I found when I landed on Charlotte soil was amazing—nothing at all like what Lord Lieutenant Cornwallis had experienced.

There was just no comparison.

It must have really stunk being him.

Where he had arrived to a hornet's nest of rebellion and military resistance, I was greeted by a host of unmet friends and a ton of warm acceptance.

In addition to the new names and faces that I'd encounter, it was as if I also had my own fan club cheering me on from near and afar. It is decidedly a very small club, but then again, I'm a very small person. Thus, a simple algebraic formula would easily conclude that that particular and completely fictitious association is proportionately occupied.

Some of those inhabitants would be in attendance at the conference. Others had offered assistance from home and from various places behind the scenes. Without backing from these movers and shakers, things would not have moved or been shaken as well as they did.

In fact, I wouldn't have even been there if it weren't for them. Happily, they served as my ground support, my base, my foundation of strength and encouragement.

Pastor Jeff Leake improved my speechwriting with an outline that offered guidance for smooth transitions from one point to the next.

My sister-in-law, Jodi, helped me with speaking tips and techniques. She was also my initial practice audience, my one-person congregation, while I rehearsed.

Even practicing in front of my own family was a daunting task. Though I knew I shouldn't, I mostly kept my eyes on my paper and just read it, verbatim, like I did in '06.

But everyone believed in me. Not only did they convey it with their words of encouragement, they clearly demonstrated that belief by their actions.

Among them is *The Band of Brothers*—a men's group to which Eric belongs. But they aren't a chess club or a book reading group. They are more like a motorcycle gang that consists of about two dozen church guys—godly, upstanding men who simply do life together and carry out good deeds for those who could use a helping hand.

Collectively, *The Brothers* paid for our travel fuel and meals.

Others went above and beyond to see that we had everything we needed and then some. Among these individuals are Mike Straub and his wife, Tiffany. To lighten our load and give us less to worry about, they drove down ahead of us, transporting my artwork and books for me to sell at my signing table.

Also there is Mark Szymanski who lobbied and campaigned (or whatever it all was that he did) to make sure our van rental and hotel accommodations were covered.

On the day of the conference, Mike and Miss Tiffany arrived early to help with setup. Mike also presented everyone with food from McDonald's, but I didn't accept any. I just wasn't much in the mood to eat by that time.

The weeks prior gave me time to prepare what I felt I should say in my presentation, but it also gave me time to become nervous about speaking in front of hundreds of people.

So, I didn't carry much of an appetite with me.

In fact, I hardly ate anything the entire weekend. The exciting atmosphere and my nerves just wouldn't allow it. I didn't want something unsightly or unladylike to happen. The only thing I wanted to come from my mouth was my speech and nothing else.

Having opted to fly down, Eric also met up with us at the conference, which was held at a ginormous church that consisted of a sprawling campus and multiple buildings. For me and my entourage, that first night consisted of just taking it all in because I wasn't scheduled to speak until the next day.

With my table set up and everything neatly organized, Eric took me on a tour of the massive facility. In true Eric fashion that only he can display so stylishly, he led me around as if he owned the place.

Our excursion began in the sanctuary, which was where my second speech would be delivered. The room was huge, and it was such a beautiful and majestic establishment.

The conference hadn't started yet. And while we were in there, a band was on stage, sound checking and running through some songs. The audio system was crazy loud.

I happen to like crazy loud.

I just couldn't believe that I was there in the thick of it all.

Eric and I began devising a plan for how we wanted things to go when it would come my time to speak. One thing was sure; I wouldn't remain in my wheelchair during my presentation.

When I reached the edge of the stage in my wheelchair and slipped off my driving arms, I climbed onto the massive platform amidst the singers and musicians. I could feel the rumble of the music, the low frequency notes thumping through my body.

I was a human subwoofer!

And no one seemed to mind that I was up there.

More acceptance, more support!

Eric and I decided it might be best if I'd just sit directly on the floor of the stage, instead of on a tabletop, which had been an initial thought. After making that determination, we then made our way to the fine arts building where I'd be delivering my opening speech to the youth. Same deal there; I'd sit directly on the stage.

The only thing that would be acutely different between the two setups pertained to the sound reinforcement technique. For my first speech, I'd be positioned in front of a mic stand with a corded microphone. In the sanctuary, I'd be fitted with a wireless headset system.

After working everything out and seeing the entire venue, it was late by the time we all headed back to the hotel. Being mixed with a potpourri of emotions such as enthusiasm, awe, and gratitude, I was as excited as I was exhausted.

And still extremely nervous.

Shortly after we returned, I was sitting outside the bathroom door while my mom was inside. Our room entrance door was to my immediate left. On the other side of it, in the hallway, I suddenly heard a hilarious proclamation.

It was the voice of a girl, passing by and calling out, "Sir, sir! Your pants are falling down!"

There's a good chance that she saw a man coming from the pool area, possibly carrying his street clothes. I felt she probably meant to say that he was dropping some of them, i.e. his pants. Whatever the explanation, by hearing that and envisioning a few sidesplitting images, it literally made me laugh out loud.

I needed a good chuckle after such a long, intense day. And I appreciated the amusement. Often underrated and easily overlooked, laughter is extremely important to healthy and productive living. So much so that the *Bible* says laughter serves as a medicine for us.

That being the case—and though I was the one laughing at the moment—I firmly hold the belief that Mom could open her own pharmacy with it.

She's an addict. Laughter is her drug of choice, keeping her sufficiently medicated at all times. But little did I know that I'd be spooning up several doses of it to her as we slept that night.

It all started with me talking in my sleep…in a nonhuman sort of way.

Actually, I was speaking whale.

Or blowing like one.

I'm often forced to do that during the daytime when my hair gets in my mouth. However you'd choose to describe my act of expelling the errant, flavorless strands, I have to spit it out, blow it, or puff it away.

Apparently, I was fighting that condition and unknowingly "blowing like a whale," after we all went to sleep.

It must have been like something straight out of *Finding Nemo*. But mine would be a PG-13 version, the sound effects thereof being much scarier than that of the original animated movie.

To my defense, I probably could argue that whale sounds are more ladylike than snoring like a warthog, but Mom found it all to be reasonably entertaining, regardless.

Then again, we're talking about Janet Brooks. What else could you expect? Forget the notion that she might have a few screws loose; some of hers are missing, altogether. It has often been suspected that we might find them in a coffee can on Dad's work bench, but it seems no one has bothered to look there. Or, maybe for a woman who is just so incessantly slap happy, it wouldn't matter if we found them or not.

As for whale calls, who would expect to hear such oceanic sounds in the city of Charlotte, landlocked more than 200 miles from the coastline?

In high school, I chose Spanish as an alternative language course. I was a quick learner and did well in it. But other than unruly hair that gets in my mouth, nothing offers a practical explanation as to how I picked up "Whale" along the way.

It may have come in the package as part of my personal aquatic theme.

The Whale Whisperer

How's that for a future movie title?

Given the shortness of my overall tallness, why not make it a miniseries?

Or not.

Mom said there were times throughout the night when she wanted to yell, "Thar she blows!"

Knowing her as I do, I could only hope she wouldn't feel compelled to do that in the middle of one of my speeches.

17

Reaching Out

By the time we arrived at the conference on Saturday morning, I was a rolling bundle of nerves—simultaneously overwhelmed, excited, and tense.

Yes, I'm quite the multi-tasker.

Fortunately, caring inhabitants greeted me.

There was not a single hornet to be found anywhere!

Not even the jersey-wearing NBA type.

Engaging in conversation with such wonderful people helped put aside my worry of giving a public speech. They stopped at my table for various reasons. Many were drawn to the slideshow that was running on my laptop. Others examined my art pieces. Some wanted to buy a book or just say hello.

All were totally supportive.

Some were just hilariously endearing.

One in particular was a boy who was about nine. He was a volunteer who came by to look at my artwork and to talk. I told him how I draw and the technique that I use for cutting out pieces by holding an X-Acto knife in my mouth. He seemed quite amazed, but he didn't cry about it like Eric had done.

The boy was also a proficient chatterbox, talking nonstop on any topic he could think of. When others came by and interrupted, he would then turn his attention to Eric and talk with him about me. At one point, he even asked Eric what grade I was in.

Eric politely explained, "Miss Amy has been out of school for quite a while."

The boy definitely made my weekend, as did an entertaining group of bubbly young dance girls.

A woman named Susie had come up and conversed with me at length. Before leaving, she mentioned this dance group that was about to perform next door in the fine arts department.

At that time, Eric was nowhere to be found, and I was waiting for him to get back from wherever it was that he had wandered off to. So, I didn't have the opportunity to attend the dance performance, as I would have liked.

Afterwards, Miss Susie returned and shadowed me the entire day, following me everywhere and offering to help in any way she could. Turns out, she was a mom to one of the dance girls, each of whom stopped by my table after their routine and quickly became fans and friends of mine.

They were all so sweet, having me sign my bookmarks for them as well as a little notebook, like the ones that we used to carry around Disney World seeking Mickey's autograph. The girls asked me an infinite number of questions. We all talked and laughed and took countless pictures together.

Their group leaders and other Igniters greatly encouraged me throughout the day and made my time there very enjoyable.

Having mentioned that it would be my first time giving a major presentation, some offered advice or said a prayer for me. I felt so loved by each of them. They had never met me before, but they treated me as if I was a member of their own family.

My first speech was to be to the youth at 1:25 that afternoon. The dance team girls couldn't wait to hear me and openly expressed eagerness about it. As the hour approached and my nervousness began to resurface, they seemed more excited about my speech than I was.

While watching the clock in anticipation, Eric likened it to waiting for the dentist.

I told him, "I think I'd rather actually *be* at the dentist's."

There's just nothing like a good root canal to take your mind off the pressures of public speaking.

I already have some parts missing. Amputate a few teeth if you'd like. You don't even have to numb me; just yank those puppies right out!

At one o'clock, we headed to the fine arts building to finish our wait. My parents prayed for me, and just before that segment of the conference was about to start, Eric prayed also.

The dance girls lined up and sat in the front row, but during the preliminary music, they all got up and left. Later, I would learn from Miss Susie that they had an additional, unscheduled performance coming up in the main sanctuary, and they had to rehearse while I gave my speech. Their dance instructor, Miss Donna, told me how upset the girls were that they had to miss it. So, afterwards, I told her they could come by my table and talk for as long as they wanted. I missed seeing them dance, they missed hearing me speak. It was ironic and unintended.

With Miss Susie

During my speech, Logic joined me and made herself at home, lying down at my side like a good girl. The kids in attendance listened intently and laughed when I made a joke. And I scarcely even looked at my notes the entire time!

Before I knew it, the first one was over.

Something Eric and I hadn't worked on the night before was a good exit strategy for me. Or if we did, I had forgotten it. All I knew was that I needed an Old West get-away, where the cowboy jumps from the rooftop, onto his motorized wheelchair, and thunders over the horizon without looking back.

No matter my method of exit or route of escape, I couldn't afford to dillydally because I had to book it over to the sanctuary to speak again at 2:00.

Eric helped me off the stage and into my arms. I then took off without stressing over the idea of entering a ginormous sanctuary and facing about half the population of our planet.

Thankfully, there just wasn't time to think about it.

As soon as I got mic'ed up with the transmitter and headset, Eric immediately assisted me onto the main stage. Logic also came and assumed her prone position next to me. I then delivered my second speech with near perfection.

Again, I barely consulted my written material. This was especially good considering the headset I was wearing. The first time I attempted to turn a page of my notes, the microphone scraped against the paper, creating a terrible rumble.

But that was my only blunder. From there on, it was smooth sailing. What amazed me the most was how calm I felt throughout.

Not comfortable, just calm.

Taking into account all the nerves I had been dealing with, it was eerie that I'd be so relaxed. But there's a perfectly rational explanation for that; God had shown up, and He took over at just the precise moment. I was fully alert to His presence and could truly feel everyone's prayers and love and unwavering support.

My speech seemed more like I was just having a normal conversation where I was the one doing all the talking.

I was merely telling my story.

Though everything unfolded in a blur of surrealism, I was intensely aware of the smallest details around me. Fortunately, it all appeared to move in slow motion. (Just my speed!)

All throughout, Logic was so cute. She would occasionally lift her head, scan the audience, and look up at me, adoringly. She appeared as though she felt she belonged there, as if we both belonged there.

One of the things I had been worrying about was that I might not have enough material to fill my time slot. As it turned out, I actually exceeded my limit by a minute and a half.

Oh well, they'd just have to cut a few commercials, right?

During the entire trip, God had given me little signs, things that aligned with what I had written in my speech. He sent droplets of encouragement from every direction, confirming that I was right where I was supposed to be and that I was carrying out His will.

There was the message on the room key. Also, on a bracelet that was given to me was an inscription that read, "**No Excuse.**" And though I don't specifically recall what it was, just before I was to speak to the youth, even Miss Susie had said something to me that was actually in my notes.

Both presentation experiences were like nothing that I could have imagined. Finally, they were over. The speeches had been delivered. My contribution was made.

I'm done!

A tide of sweet relief washed over me.

It would now be time to just have some fun.

Up next was the dance team. Though they had been out rehearsing and didn't hear either of my speeches, I would finally get to watch their routine. Not only was I eager to see it, my immediate objective was to quickly disappear into the audience and allow the focus of attention to be shifted onto the girls.

Again, I tried to flee the scene as fast as possible. Though everything had gone much better than I could have hoped, I still wanted to run and hide—to hop into my wheelchair, burn rubber, and escape as if absconding with the offering plate.

As Eric assisted, he whispered to me to relax, slow down, and take my time. But I couldn't; a weight had been lifted!

I felt lighter.

And grateful.

I appreciated Eric's help. I was thankful to Dad and Mom for everything they had sacrificed to get me there. Inwardly, I was thanking God for the strength that He had given, and everyone else for their support, encouragement, and various contributions.

The best part is the realization that most of it is stuff that I can offer to others. I can give it back or pay it forward. I can be there to talk or to listen or to send up a prayer. I can continue to reach out, and I wouldn't need arms to do it.

Eventually, I was told something that truly humbled me. In my rush to get away, in my concentrated effort to vanish after speaking, I hadn't even noticed it.

Unless the response was all in his imagination, Eric informed me that—at the conclusion of my speeches—the audience gave me a standing ovation. Try as I might, this is something I suppose I can never repay.

18

Electrical Shock

Though I did fairly well in it, math was never my favorite subject throughout school. So, help me if you would. I'd like us to do a little addition together.

The use of calculators, pencils and paper, or old-fashioned adding machines are fully permitted and strongly encouraged. You may even total it in the margin of this page. Or, if you really want to impress me, simply count on your fingers and toes.

For those who have been following closely, you should be able to correctly answer this question: *How many times has my friend, Eric, been struck by lightning?*

No matter the calculation method, your answer, if worked correctly, should repeatedly sum to a simple single digit. It's kind of like an algebraic expression that is raised to the zero power; the answer is always one.

Is that what you came up with? Did you get "one" as an answer? You should have because that's it. Eric has been struck by lightning just once. Only one measly time.

What's the big deal, right? For the most part, he got over it just fine. As he mentioned, it was actually a benefit, a bonus feature, an old fallback excuse to use with Miss Heidi. Lucky him.

But he was zapped only one time, no more. Remember that.

If this were another campaign, I believe I'd have a leg up on my competitor. Well, I would if I had a leg.

I make this claim because I've experienced this sensation multiple times. Not an all-out, upon-further-review, official lightning strike, per se, but something similar enough to qualify. To keep track of them would be impossible, as they were frequent and innumerable. Regardless of the weather condition, it happens almost always when I go outdoors for exercise.

Picture the scene in the classic underdog movie, *Rocky*. While training for his unprecedented fight against heavyweight champion Apollo Creed, character Rocky Balboa runs up the stairs at the Philadelphia Museum of Art and does a celebratory dance at the top. That's me. That's what I do— in a generic, off brand sort of way.

Whereas Rocky ran up the stairway in Philly, I scoot up and down our back porch ramp in Pittsburgh. For me it's the same thing. Close enough anyway. And so much so that, if I can improve my jab and overall reach a little, I just might film a seven-part "Amy Balboa" series someday.

In resemblance to Eric's lightning strike are the electrical jolts that I receive when I do my ramp workouts. Apparently, it's a bad combination. Part of the cause is that the ramp isn't made of real wood; it's a manufactured composite. It's the good stuff that doesn't produce splinters. Lucky me.

But as my clothes slide beneath me and create friction against the surface, I often receive hip-stinging, bum-tingling strikes of static electricity. Sometimes they are so intense that I'm forced to abandon my exercise efforts, altogether. If I could have somehow captured this static, I would now be marketing my own brand of lightning in a bottle.

Mathematically, my jolts have outnumbered Eric's by at least a bazillion—give or take a few. So, you'd think I'd be used to it by now, possibly even immune. But I'm not.

One particular shock I received has affected me from the very moment that it struck. Conversely, unlike Eric and his short-term memory loss and systems overload, I was fortunate enough to have retained full recall of things that I had known.

For example, I do recall that it was the legendary Major Leaguer, Lawrence Peter "Yogi" Berra, who said, "This is like déjà vu all over again."

I can relate. Like Yogi, I too have had a déjà vu all over again. And in more ways than just the static charges.

Both were extremely significant.

The first segment is recorded in *Unseen Arms*. It occurred after I had just received my first service dog and was completing my freshman year of school. Just when I thought life couldn't possibly get any better after receiving Jade, I was then hit with the shattering surprise of a free trip to Walt Disney World.

Jade and Disney, back-to-back blessings! Unbelievable!

And yet, these many years later, something as astonishing would unfold before me in comparable fashion. It happened on a Monday evening, February 24, 2014, less than twenty-four hours after returning from my speaking engagement in Charlotte.

Though tired and tender in body, I was in especially high spirits and amazed by the incredible experiences of the weekend.

Mom and Dad shared those sentiments.

As part of the same trip, I had also accepted an invitation to speak at a little Methodist church in Thomasville, North Carolina, on our way home, on Sunday. My speech there went as well as the others did at the Ignite conference.

At neither venue did I fall on my face or stink up the meetings in any way. To reference the aforementioned rodeo analogy, I wasn't bucked out of the arena or trampled beneath any thundering hoofs. Nor was I lassoed, hog tied, or hauled away in a cattle truck. More than having just survived the weekend and my speeches, I had thrived, throughout!

Mom and Dad were feeling better, and even Logic seemed to figure out that we had accomplished a task and would return to life as she had known it. All was well, and I couldn't wish for anything more. I was expecting nothing but to recoup a bit and get back into a normal routine.

As shocks often do, this other, more substantial one came electronically. It had nothing to do with fake wood or fabric or Rocky Balboa workouts; it happened inside my computer. But there's no need to be alarmed; everything is properly grounded. And as far as I can tell, we are in no immediate threat of an electrical fire.

What I'm referring to is something completely different. It wasn't the usual electrical shock as such. Fortunately, it involved no skin burns, scorched clothing, or singed eyebrows. This particular jolt was strictly confined to my emotions.

My heart was completely defibrillated by it.

Arriving via email and landing in my 'In' box on that particular evening was a song lyric pasted into the message field. There was an audio file attached. The subject title read, *Unseen Arms, the Musical*.

I called for Mom and Dad to come. With them huddled with me at my computer, I double-clicked the attachment. The sound that emitted from my speakers and the words that I read on the screen stunned me beyond belief.

The song—one that was written about me—was titled from my book. It made me cry. Mom too. Maybe even Dad a little, but I'm not sure, and I'm not going to ask him. Mom immediately requested that I "record" the song on her "doflunky." (The translation was that she wanted me to download it onto her iPod).

The full reality of receiving the song was that I had just returned from an amazing trip and received standing ovations for a couple of fifteen-minute speeches. It seemed nothing could beat that. It was more than I deserved. And now this!

Like the incredible gift of Jade followed by the miraculous trip to Disney World, I had, comparatively, experienced a miraculous trip and received an incredible gift.

Don't tell Eric, but it seems lightning does strike twice in the same place. In other words, déjà vu can happen all over again. A man called Yogi knew all about that. As do I!

19

Musically Challenged

I f you found the earlier quote by Leonardo da Vinci—about his work offending God and man—to be somewhat intriguing, here's one that's guaranteed to challenge the riddle-solving sector of your brain:

The beatings will continue until the music improves.

Interesting, no?

Take a guess at who said it.

Wait! That isn't a hint; *The Who* didn't say it.

As we cue the *Jeopardy* theme song, I'll present your answer choices:

A) Luther Vandross

B) Van Morrison

C) Jon Bon Jovi

D) Johaan van Beethoven

You have only thirty-four seconds. This will also provide a chance for you to redeem yourself if you missed the mathematic question about Eric and his rather odd propensity toward playing with lightning bolts.

But hurry!

Time's running out!

Pencils down! Sorry.

Do you think you circled the correct answer?

I have to admit that it could be considered a trick question. As far as I know, there isn't solid proof that he did say it, other than for the tee shirt that it was printed on. And it wasn't from any that Myia and I had made.

Hence, the validity might be dependent upon how much trust we place in the manufacturers of casual summer attire. But according to that tee shirt, the quotation was credited to Johaan van Beethoven.

The answer is D.

Don't let it bother you if you happened to get it wrong. You won't find anyone more musically challenged than me. Can you really picture Amy Brooks holding a piano recital or busting out a heavy-metal drum solo? I do love music, but when it comes down to it, I really can't tell the difference between a key change and a key ring. And that's more true than falsetto.

Either way, let's move on.

Assuming Johaan truly did say that, to what was he referring, exactly? Was he beating himself up? Tearing himself down? Like da Vinci, was he criticizing his work?

Could he have been speaking of someone else and suggesting something completely different? Was he addressing a deeper, darker, more literal meaning?

As the father of the infamous Ludwig, did Johaan use corporal punishment to advance the development of his son's music compositions?

It's something to think about.

Consider it a challenge.

Or, you could choose to give it no thought, whatsoever, and simply enjoy the beauty of music. That's what Brett Barry does.

But more than simply enjoying music, Brett creates it, exquisitely. As a professional musician, he writes and records and performs with nothing short of excellence.

I know this factually because it was Brett who recorded my song. It was his composing abilities, smooth finger-picking, warm guitar sound, and rich, strong vocals that created *Unseen Arms* and brought it to life, musically.

Brett is a veteran of his craft and another artist that I've added to my list of favorites. It just so happens that his type of art is expressed in lyrical structure, melodic arrangements, and various forms of public performances, studio productions, and other technical works.

If you're up for a real musical challenge, Brett can provide it. His energy and passion will inspire you. His lyrics will stir your soul. His convictions will move you to action. His songs will challenge you to understand what "*Worship Is*," that it's "the only thing you take with you when you go."

Brett is extremely talented, well-traveled, and highly accomplished. Though not all are still available, to date he has recorded eight albums— all of which are Christ-centered, one being relationship oriented. Among those projects, Brett has recorded a Christmas album! And he currently has two new albums in the works.

What's most important is that Brett is a solid Christian, a dedicated husband to Erin, and a loving, much involved father of a daughter and two sons.

The older boy is named Brooks!

Cool, huh?

It would be even cooler if his middle name was Orpik, but Sidney Crosby wouldn't think so.

Though I haven't met Miss Erin or Brooks or his sister, Laurén, I've been blessed to meet Brett and the youngest of the Barry siblings, Pierz. I actually got to hang out with them. Not that I would have chosen otherwise, but I didn't really have much say in the matter—seeing how they both just happened to appear in our living room, seemingly out of nowhere.

It happened late in the morning of June 26, 2014.

Mom informed me ahead of time that we could expect visitors on that morning. Jeff would be coming over. He's my biographer/ghostwriter guy. Miss Ginny would be accompanying him. She's the wife of said biographer/ghostwriter guy.

For them, I would have rolled out of bed and thrown on anything, but Mom alluded to a possible surprise guest as well.

So, I got myself completely dolled up and totally babed out.

Well, I at least slid into a dress and ran my head beneath a hairbrush. But I didn't know who was coming. She said my guest would be a surprise. And a surprise he was—Brett and Pierz both.

First, I had to get over the shock of who had just shown up and the amazement that he'd drive all the way from…well…from wherever it was that he and Pierz had come. I couldn't believe how my parents had kept it a secret, but they really pulled a good one over on me with that. And what an awesome time it was!

I quickly discovered that Brett and Pierz are so down-to-earth friendly, sincere, humble, and easy to talk to. If I had to choose one word to accurately describe them, it would be "genuine."

Together, we all talked and laughed and prayed.

Mom made lasagna for lunch. So, we also pigged out a little.

For four months, Brett had been a bit of a mystery man. He was a name on an email, a face on the Internet, a voice on a song—on lots of songs, but especially on one that was written about me. But there is much more about him than that.

Of the many great qualities in Brett Barry, one is that he is so amazingly similar to Eric in terms of compassion, selfless action, humor, and intelligence. The list goes on. It's like those guys are the same person, minus the tattoos—crayon drawn or otherwise—because Brett doesn't have a tatted sleeve like Eric (and me).

Just as Eric had once asked my mom why I didn't have working limbs, Brett had also asked Jeff that very question.

Mom's answer to Eric and Jeff's to Brett was identical—that I couldn't afford them and that they aren't included in my insurance coverage.

That wasn't an acceptable answer for either of the men, and both set out to do something about it. Eric established *Arms Around Amy*, and Brett recorded *Unseen Arms*.

Somehow these guys are twins, miraculously born to different parents, five years and 2,500 miles apart.

Plus a few months and a mile or two.

One was born in Pennsylvania, the other in Oregon. A cop here, a musician there. And that's basically where their differences end. To remain in good favor with Mr. Owles at Joshua Tree Publishing, I won't use up a lot of his printing ink by listing all the other things. But to sum it up, the mold from which these men are poured is one that was formed in the shape of the cross of Christ.

This couldn't have been made more evident on the morning of Brett's visit. Before he left that day, he cracked open a guitar case that he had carried in with him. From inside it, he removed an Epiphone guitar. And from the living room of our home, while seated next to me on our sofa, he played *Unseen Arms*—live, in person, and with perfection.

Where are those standing ovation abilities when I really, really need them?

A smile and a thank you seemed all too insufficient, but that was all I could offer.

When he entered our home, Brett was a resident of the state of Maryland, a husband and father, a singer, a songwriter, a musician. He walked in a man of distinction, an individual of essence. Part stranger, part celebrity.

By the time he and Pierz drove off, a single word quickly surfaced that truly defines who Brett Barry is.

No Jeopardy theme song required.

No multiple-choice question needed.

There is nothing challenging about it.

To me, to my family, to my home, he is "friend."

*With Brett and Jeff ~ a rose
between two thorns or a monkey in the middle?*

20

Thoughts In Motion

Where do they come from? Whether we remember it or not, we've all asked that question. Some of us may not admit it, but everyone has made that inquiry.

We were probably about four or five when—in our naivety and innocence—we simply blurted it out to our parents, no matter where we were or who was around. You might have been a bit older, but I'm sure you presented the question at some point during your childhood. Maybe you just don't remember.

If Dad walked away—pretending like he didn't know—or if Mom blushed and turned her head, you probably inquired of a friend, while casually skipping rope or playing recklessly with toy trucks.

There's nothing to be ashamed of. Our minds were growing. Our imaginations were expanding. Our thoughts were running all over the place.

We were young, observant, and inquisitive. Right?

There's no need for any embarrassment.

It's a perfectly acceptable topic.

Totally normal.

Completely natural.

100%.

No preservatives added.

Maybe you are still pondering, trying to figure it out.

That's okay; trust me. Everyone has wondered. Each of us has asked that all-consuming question. Come on, be honest. We all want to know: *Where do songs come from?*

I know what you're thinking; mine came from an email attachment. But where do they come from in general? If you don't know the answer, I believe I can offer some insight. And we don't have to be shy or make a thing of it. I promise it won't be weird or uncomfortable for you. But first, we must dispel of any myths or false notions that you've been carrying.

Regardless of what your parents or playground buddies may have told you, songs are not delivered by a slow-flying, low-altitude music stork. And songs don't simply grow on magical melody trees somewhere on the edge of Nashville.

I do humbly admit that I've learned a few things about writing since venturing into this "author" thing. And since you are likely taking notes and hanging on my every word, I'm sure you'll want to jot this down: *Songs are created by writing them.*

Pretty deep, isn't it?

And what's even deeper is the story behind my song, how it landed in my email having never been out in public—still in the package, still wrapped in cellophane, as it were.

If the song had come with a cost, the price tag would have still been attached. Though, to me, it was laundry-fresh and sparkling new, I would learn that it was already three years old—or that long in the making—by the time it came along and shocked me as it did.

Please, allow me to turn the tables for a moment. Jeff has helped me tell my story. Now I am insistent upon telling his. Yet, it's all part of mine because it's the backstory on how my song came about.

The whole thing started with a statement Mom made to Jeff toward the very beginning of us writing my first book.

Prior to working with me, Jeff had mostly worked with men, taller, stronger, and more able-bodied than me. He consulted with professional athletes about writing. He turned down offers to write for a couple of different NASCAR drivers. And he almost landed a writing gig with an extreme balancer in Norway.

Jeff also had been writing for a man in Texas, who is a lot like Eric—a fast-paced, hardcore, over-achiever. The man was also a decorated Special Forces soldier who was highly trained, battle tested, and tough as nails—

the kind of guy who might eat a grizzly bear for lunch and use its bones for a toothpick.

He and Jeff stayed busy. In addition to the writing work, they remained active in other ways, did guy stuff, kept moving—did some traveling around, some hanging out, and enjoyed a few recreational activities together.

And then, along comes Amy Brooks.

Consider the contrast—me being a shy, quiet, thirty-two-inch, stay-at-home female civilian without human limbs and no professional-grade athleticism. I'm not as well balanced as the Norwegian guy. I live my life much quieter than a 725-horse racing engine. And I've never acquired a taste for grizzly meat.

Like the doctors of my past, Jeff was quietly wondering how to work with someone of my specific category.

The first time he hugged me, the embrace was practically non-existent. It was as if he thought I might crumble into a pile of tiny pieces, leaving him with a mess to sweep up and some explaining to do.

He entered our working relationship cautiously, choosing to begin by conducting multiple telephone interviews with Mom, and some with Dad. His method of approach was to gather information on my infancy and to allow me time to get to know him as a writer, then as a person, and eventually as someone who just won't go away.

Apparently, Jeff watches too many of those real-life, true-crime shows, where the narrators all reveal an identical method for solving a case or catching a criminal.

Ask Eric; he'll tell you. Every detective will confirm it. Any investigator will say the same thing: they simply go where the evidence leads them.

According to Jeff, inspired writing is similar.

But instead of following muddy tracks and fingerprints, he pursues the fallen breadcrumbs of inspiration. He goes where it leads him. That's how my song began.

When he and Mom were talking, she dropped one of those morsels. Though it was unintentional, her comment was quite moving and couldn't be ignored. It was one of those of the "must-follow" variety.

Her words reached into Jeff's heart and squeezed a little. But she wasn't even aware of it. He didn't comment. He didn't respond. Not verbally, anyway.

After that talk, Jeff didn't sit down to write as one might expect. Instead, he was on his feet, working with his hands, engaging in physical labor. He claims that he often thinks better under those conditions.

This seems a bit odd for a writer, for someone whose work involves sitting motionlessly in a cushioned leather swivel chair, tapping at a computer keyboard. But I won't mention it if you don't. Besides, his thinking method seems to be effective.

While working and walking and moving about, Mom's comment continually ran through his thoughts. "As a mom," she had said, "I can't help but to worry about how Amy's life will be when Rich and I are no longer here."

The stirring behind those words compelled Jeff to pen a song lyric, titled *Unseen Arms*.

That's where the inspiration led him.

Like anything deemed worthwhile, the song creation wouldn't be easy, and it wouldn't happen swiftly. In fact, it almost didn't happen at all.

After scribbling out the words and, later, revising them, Jeff composed music for it on his guitar. But the results were not to his satisfaction. Similar to how he had followed the inspiration that led him to write it, his gut instinct told him the music didn't compliment the lyric as it should.

But he was stuck with it, with the same internal "guide melody" to which he had written the words. And there was no escaping that particular sound, which "just wasn't quite right."

He then set it aside.

From time to time, he would pull the song out and pick at it like a dish of mysterious leftovers. But it was always cold and stale. So, he did what any normal guy would do with crusty old leftovers—put it back in the fridge, so to speak.

That's what he did, and that's where it stayed.

It seemed, in Jeff's opinion, the more attention he gave the song the worse it became. Even the words began to demand another re-write in certain areas, but he didn't bother because of the musical rut in which the song was entrenched.

Jeff then consulted a professional music friend. The idea was that he would pay a qualified musician to compose new and better music and provide a demo-like recording of it—for no reason but to present the song as a gift to my parents and me. It would serve as a reminder that God will forever hold me in His unseen arms, that I'll be okay no matter what.

After a year of waiting with no results or follow-up, he contacted a second music friend and waited another year or so. Both musicians had been interested in helping with the song, but were simply unable to fit it into their schedules. All the while, Jeff worked with me, writing my book, but kept the pending song a secret. He even began to doubt if it would ever come into actual existence.

As for my book title, you have probably noticed a similarity between it and my song. Of course, this wasn't coincidental, but it also wasn't something Jeff had planned. Though he had always thought Unseen Arms would be a good book title for me, he never suggested it as we compiled the manuscript.

As the book's author, he felt the title should be mine to create. Titling such a project is personal and powerful. It generates a brand and a unique identity. Being my story, it was my place and privilege to title it. But as some of you may know, I tend to be a slacker at times.

Occasionally, Jeff would ask if I had chosen a book title. I hadn't. As my manuscript neared completion, he asked again.

Nope, nada.

Finally, we were ready to be published, and my book remained nameless. So, he asked yet again. (Didn't I tell you he was someone who just won't go away?)

As it turned out, I still didn't have a title. That's when he offered "Unseen Arms." I loved it. And I still had no idea that there was a possible song in the works, one that almost ended up in Jeff's "songwriting junkyard."

Apparently, everyone has one of those.

The thing that saved it from being filed there is that Jeff likes to exercise. And he doesn't need a wheelchair ramp to do it. Fortunately, he owns a treadmill, which he uses frequently. Of course, to look at the guy, you'd never guess it.

But I won't mention that, either.

I'll just say, physical evidence might suggest that the majority of Jeff's running is done from his couch to the dinner table, the distance of which is motivated by Miss Ginny's excellent cooking.

Be that as it may, shortly after my finished manuscript was submitted to the publisher, Jeff descended into his basement for a run. As someone who thinks well while in motion, it would be a time to contemplate and reflect.

Over the space of the past two and one-half years—as much as possible—we had worked on my book. And now, it was done. Jeff felt a sense of accomplishment and satisfaction. Like me, he was grateful that we were soon to be published, but something was missing; it was the musical expression of my story. So, he was feeling a bit melancholy about that, about the failed attempts to produce my song.

I have little expertise when it comes to motorized workout equipment. My thing is to just not get electrocuted when doing a simple calorie burn. But I assume Jeff stepped onto his treadmill, primed the carburetor, yanked the pull cord, and fired up its powerful Hemi V-8 engine (imported from Detroit).

I'm told his model is a nice one. He claims the machine can actually run by itself. All Jeff has to do is keep up with it.

Besides the Hemi, the contraption is equipped with the latest Internet capabilities and other contemporary features. The display has a "Maps" setting (so he doesn't get lost). I think it even has a GPS (to offer him the quickest route back to the dinner table).

Most significant of Jeff's treadmill is that it has an onboard stereo. As a lifelong music enthusiast, that's the only way he likes to exercise—while jamming to upbeat "tuneage." (Probably *Rocky* soundtracks on most days.)

On this particular afternoon, however, he chose a different music selection and did so rather nonchalantly. For more than twenty years, Jeff had been a Brett Barry fan. And it was Brett's music that he just happened to choose at the moment, for no other reason than that it had been a long time since he had listened to any of Brett's work.

During that run, as Brett sang, inspiration struck. But it was disguised as the quirkiest, most ridiculous idea Jeff had ever had: *Contact Brett Barry to compose the music for Unseen Arms.*

Wherever the idea had come from, it was absurd. It was ludicrous. It was a completely moronic notion. The only reason he didn't laugh out loud was because he couldn't draw enough air into his lungs to do so.

Panting like a dog and sweating like a pig, Jeff continued running in an attempt to chase the preposterous idea completely out of his thoughts. Obviously, he isn't in too good of shape because it seems he didn't run quite fast enough.

Then again, he is a grandpa.

21

Icing

For those of you who are not hockeyologists and have often wondered what an "icing" call is, I'll be glad to help you understand it. (I came through okay with explaining where songs come from, right?)

Icing is a rules violation that essentially occurs when—in a single motion—a team shoots the puck across the red line at center ice, beyond the blue line in the opposing team's zone, and past their goal line.

When this happens, the officials blow their whistle to stop the play. The puck is then returned for a faceoff in the zone from where the puck was iced.

This act of "dumping the puck" was deemed an infraction to prevent a team from running time off the game clock in such a manner.

But there are a few exceptions to this rule, conditions under which icing is "waved off," meaning it is allowed. No whistle blown. No stoppage in play.

Exception #1– Icing is permitted if the team that iced the puck is skating short-handed, due to having a player in the penalty box.

Exception #2– Icing is permitted if the opposing goalie touches the puck that was dumped into his zone.

Exception #3– Icing is permitted if the team that dumped the puck is the first down the ice to touch it.

Exception #4– Icing is permitted if you are a professional singer/songwriter/musician whose name is Brett Barry.

You might have trouble finding that last one in the official NHL rules book, but it's true, nonetheless. Though Brett appears well cut and physically fit, he has never played in the National Hockey League. But he is a personal exception, and my song would not exist if it weren't for him.

Though Jeff was struggling to determine if he was coming to his senses or completely losing them, by the end of his run that day, he decided there'd be no harm visiting Brett's website at brettbarry.com to present his ridiculous idea to the man, via email.

As with the other two musicians prior, Jeff asked if Brett would consider a onetime composing project for hire. He shared my story with Brett and explained how he wanted to give the song as a gift to my family, but admitted that the music was inadequate.

Brett was all in. So, maybe Jeff's idea hadn't been such a boneheaded one, after all. But don't be quick to think he's a genius, as one major flaw did exist in his intentions; it was the "for hire" part. Brett didn't accept the project as a business proposal but rather as a partnership. His involvement would be a shared gift with Jeff to us—no charge, no negotiation, no layaway plan.

Four months later, the song, *Unseen Arms*, landed in my email. Brett had written the music, further developed the lyrics, and recorded the song. All the while, I knew nothing about it.

Even now, I remain shocked by that. Unlike Eric recovering from his wimpy little lightning strike, I'm not sure I'll ever get over it completely. Nor do I want to. Brett's visit to our home came an additional four months after the song arrived.

This is where I'm the one who really needs the use of a calculator to total all the blessings.

The song file was only the beginning. Brett playing the song live in my home was an extra. (I learned that he had driven from Fredrick, Maryland, more than 200 miles away. That in itself was an added gift.) Now, in my deepest infomercial voice, I must excitedly announce, *But wait, there's more!*

Before he and Pierz ended their visit, Brett also borrowed my laptop to show a song video that he had been working on.

I'll give you three guesses as to what song the video was of.

That too was Jeff's idea, but like the song itself, Brett not only made it happen; he went to extremes with it.

During their behind-my-back scheming and composing sessions, Jeff had suggested to Brett, one day, that maybe he could make a simple video recording of the song. Because it hadn't yet been recorded, Jeff thought it might be cool if Brett would set up a camera, so "Amy would have a face to go with the voice."

Obviously, Brett put his thoughts in motion also. Like the song, he really went big with the camera suggestion, making an all-out, full-on, professional music video!

His son, Brooks, was heavily involved in the production also. (A quick YouTube search will prove that Brooks Barry is quite an accomplished filmmaker. And he's hilarious.)

The finished product of the *Unseen Arms* music video is phenomenal. Not only does it feature Brett performing the song, it also includes still photos from my book and some of my rolling footage (referred to as such because, in it, I'm rolling.) But my favorite part is toward the end, where Miss Erin, Brooks, and Pierz also appear, dancing and hamming it up together.

But the video wasn't produced for casual viewing pleasure or for me to merely possess as a keepsake; the annotations urge the public to visit my website and purchase my book.

And then, there's the download!

Brett made the song available on iTunes with 100% of the proceeds being allocated to support my speaking ministry! I can only imagine that the amount of time and work invested by Brett and Brooks into recording the song and producing the video is immeasurable. Certainly, their generosity is also.

Added to this, Brett has shared my story with his audiences and has included my song in his set list.

Putting it into proper perspective, this is a song that almost didn't happen. It could have easily been discarded, given up on, abandoned like I initially was at birth. But I was miraculously rescued, and so was the song.

When Brett was commended for his selflessness, his gracious involvement, his unwavering commitment to all things Amy, he responded with an answer as profound as Mom's statement that had inspired it all, three years earlier.

"You know how it is when God lays something on your heart," he said. "You can say no, but you can't say no with peace."

(I think a man in the *Bible* named Jonah would surely agree.)

Well said, Brett. I could not have countered with such sophistication, which is the very thing that I've struggled with—finding a way to express myself in all that's happened.

I'm an author because this is my story, or rather the story God has made of my life. The material is assigned to my existence. My name is on the book. My picture is on the cover.

But I'm not a practicing writer.

These overwhelming circumstances have left me at a loss for words. I don't know the appropriate adjectives to express how blessed I am and how grateful I feel.

I had already received so much. My world had completely flipped upside down. Before *Unseen Arms* was even in print, my publisher requested a second manuscript.

Afterwards, I could not have imagined how that, as my first book sold, new chapters would begin to unfold in my life. I would never have fathomed that the pages would turn and doors would open as they have.

I held book signings and media interviews.

Speaking offers came in.

I was a guest on radio shows and an evening television news broadcast.

Never could I have imagined how this would only be the beginning, that I'd find myself awash in such wonderful opportunities to reach out to others.

From there, it seems God just opened the floodgates of goodness upon me.

The song was written.

Brett has sung it publicly and promoted my story.

The music video was produced.

The download is available.

The only thing I've been able to say of these above-and-beyond blessings is that everything is icing on the cake.

All infractions are waved off. Remember…

Exception #4– Icing is permitted if you are a professional singer/songwriter/musician whose name is Brett Barry.

In his home studio, Brett singing "Unseen Arms"
brettbarry.com

22

Heigh-Ho, Heigh-Ho

Resolute to my kinship with Dopey from *Snow White and the Seven Dwarfs*, it would seem fitting that I should venture off to work as he and the others did. But don't look for me to be swinging a pickaxe deep inside a diamond mine, as those jobs are likely all taken.

Yet, I have found work…in an Amy sort of way. But it isn't a typical job, as such, and it doesn't compensate in a paycheck sort of way. It is well-balanced bartering, the trading of services for the gaining of knowledge and experience.

On the morning of my visit from Jeff and Miss Ginny and Brett and Pierz, I was up early. Not only was I anticipating the arrival of my guests, I was also elbow deep with preparations for a significant book signing, to be held later that evening.

What made this appearance extra meaningful was that it would be my first on my own turf, in my own 'hood—held at the Avalon Public Library—mere blocks from our home. It would also include me sharing a verbal presentation.

Many people who I actually knew would be there.

Prior to that date, Jodi contacted *The Pittsburgh Post-Gazette*, and they ran a story about the upcoming event.

On the date of the published article, I awoke to a social media message from a man named Alex Jones, a professional photographer who owns SteelGate Studio on Pittsburgh's South Side.

Alex had read the piece about my book signing and invited me to attend a free workshop that he would be hosting for people with disabilities who might be interested in his field. The workshop was scheduled for the Saturday morning after my library appearance.

Though I did appreciate the offer, I respectfully declined for two reasons: I wasn't sure if I held a strong enough interest in photography to formally study it. More importantly, I had promised my niece, Grace, a sleepover on that Friday night.

Grace had been begging me for several weeks to do a sleepover together, but I had been consumed with various obligations and busy getting ready for the book signing. So, I promised, after it was over, she could come and get all the Aunt Amy time she could handle. We would do lots of fun girl stuff, such as arts and crafts, watching movies, sunning, and swimming.

After the workshop was held, Alex messaged again to say that the gathering had been a success, and he was pleased with the overall results. As we communicated, he asked if there were any special adaptations that I use for my artwork or other tasks.

I told him I don't have any adaptations, but that I use a Wacom Intuous 4 Professional Pen Tablet for my drawings. (These tablets must be interfaced with a computer to run the software. My specific model also utilizes the computer's monitor because it isn't designed with one of its own.)

Alex referenced the Cintiq model with the luxury and convenience of containing an embedded computer screen that you draw on, directly.

I had seen them. Those specific tablets are incredibly nice. Of course, they all run off a computer, but using the Cintiq would mean I wouldn't have to watch the computer screen while drawing on the tablet, which had always been a distraction for me.

I told Alex how I'd love to have one, but like anything of such quality, they are also quite pricey. He then informed me that he had one that he wasn't using and said I could borrow it if I liked.

He also offered to schedule me for a complimentary photo shoot to strengthen my portfolio and to help with my marketing approach and overall promotion of my book and artwork.

To capture a full array of great shots, Alex wanted to make a full day of it. Thus, he inquired about the kind of food my parents and I like and asked if there were any accommodations that needed to be made for me in order for us all to enjoy lunch together at his studio on the day of the shoot.

Less than a week later, Mom and Dad and Logic and I arrived at SteelGate—a quaint, rustic upstairs studio, positioned atop the historic Terminal Building across the river from downtown.

The entire property is exceptionally appealing. Though the structures have been renovated and converted into offices, small business establishments, and warehouse spaces, the setting maintains its original rugged industrial feel.

I loved the place immediately, especially the studio itself, with its partial-brick/partial-wood flooring...some walls of brick...others of unfinished plaster...lights hanging everywhere.

It's beautiful.

Being a connection point between road, river, and rail, wandering trains rumble very closely past the place. I love that too because we live near train tracks as well, and I've developed a fondness for trains in general.

Alex and his wife, Miss Janice, are business partners at SteelGate and run the studio as a sole proprietorship. While they have no actual "employees," they do have a small group of very talented people who help them maintain a successful operation. Two, in particular, are Miss Susie, who is a hair stylist and makeup artist, and Miss Kristi, who is an accomplished photographer in her own right, with her own client list.

Before long, we got down to business. It began with a hair and makeup session for me with Miss Susie. It was a pleasant and unusual experience being made over like a cover model or some kind of celebrity knockoff.

But when the photo session began, I felt a bit awkward because I'm not the relaxed type in front of a camera and don't especially like having my picture taken. Still I have to admit, it was all very fun in spite of myself.

Alex and Miss Kristi tag-teamed on my session. Both are real pros. (Neither would have had any trouble shooting hockey action photos beyond the protective netting—something I've apparently not gotten over yet, since I'm mentioning it again.)

They also snapped shots of Logic who seemed much more comfortable in front of the camera than I did. She looked completely natural without any makeup, and she was beautiful, even though she didn't get her hair done.

Some girls are just lucky like that—camera-ready without effort.

After Logic's photos, Mom and Dad were brought up for a few glamour shots—presumably saving them for last in case they'd break the camera. Like Logic, they too passed on Miss Susie's magical studio touchups.

Probably wouldn't have helped much, anyhow.

Mom would like us to think it's because you can't improve "perfect," but I wouldn't believe her if I were you. Whatever the reason, they chose to be photographed "au naturel."

That means going without makeup, right?

I'd hate to imagine it meaning anything else. After all, Alex and Miss Janice run a clean, reputable studio, and it would only be proper for us to leave the place the way that we found it. So, we did. And the entire photo shoot was pleasant.

Lunch was also.

Alex is a stickler for details and did everything he could to make us feel comfortable and welcomed. He even remembered that I had mentioned plastic utensils are easier for me to use and that I like lemon in my water.

At the end of the shoot, Alex offered me one of his Photoshop seats, which is the number of times software can be downloaded on different devices under the same license. He had a seat open and said I could use it. Though I did have a longtime interest in learning Photoshop, I didn't want to accept this extended generosity with everything he had already done.

For years, I had been using a free software download called GIMP that is similar to Photoshop, and I was content with it. After Alex convinced me to accept the Photoshop seat, we headed out.

But we left the Cintiq tablet.

Alex walked us to the elevators and then realized we had forgotten it. He sent us down, went back for the tablet, and met us downstairs so he could send it home with me.

I believe it was the next day, when Alex and I were messaging, that he suggested ways where I could involve myself with things that I enjoy while working from home. Included in these are a demand for photo retouchers and social media administrators.

As a matter of fact, I had noticed a deficiency in his studio's social media marketing. Since I do fairly well at that type of work, I offered the idea of interning with him in exchange for Photoshop lessons. But I was thinking about the mere basics of the software so I could possibly use it to better my artwork, not for editing photos.

Alex quickly developed bigger ideas: I could improve and manage his social media page, and he could show me how to use the Photoshop software to its full potential and learn professional photo editing.

Our ideas built from there.

He would teach me the aspects of his business, and I could utilize my particular computer skills as part of his team. SteelGate is an establishment where each person contributes by using their personal talents. As puzzling as I am at times, I'd simply bring another piece of the puzzle. More appealing was that I could learn and work from the comfort of my home.

And that was it; I had negotiated a position with SteelGate Studio. Without the slightest hint of hesitation, Alex announced, "It's yours!"

Really? I have a job?

Are you pulling my leg?

Wait…you couldn't be.

Alex welcomed me aboard, accommodating to the fact that I had other obligations that would take priority over the internship. And we both began to fill our roles, completely—Alex: mentor, Amy: tormentor.

But Alex has been very patient and understanding in answering my endless string of questions. He has offered any information he can and has fully included me in all aspects of the business. Before long, I found myself learning more than I ever thought I would, and I've been able to do so at my own pace.

Having successfully synced Alex's studio computers with mine, I control them, remotely, from home, using LogMeIn software. Amongst various assignments and continued learning, I often assist Alex with his photo shoots.

Basically, I logon and look in like some sort of digital stalker. With a camera feed from the studio, I offer a pair of over-the-shoulder eyeballs by monitoring the session for him.

Maybe the shots are starting to run dark, for example. Or, there might be too much exposure. On rare occasions, a cable or fraction of lighting equipment has been known to sneak in and photobomb a shot.

Whatever the case, if I notice anything questionable with the picture quality or identify a compromise with the subject, I alert Alex by phone to his earbud where only he can hear my report.

I let him know if he needs to make any adjustments, which aids in keeping the session moving forward. This also helps reduce editing time or subsequent touch-ups, later on. Often at the end, I'll go through the hundreds of photos he's taken and narrow them down to a certain amount, depending on the nature of the shoot.

My progression with SteelGate has been such that Alex soon stopped referring to me as an intern. He also stopped referring to me as Amy and assigned me the nickname "Oracle."

That's me in my studio persona.

Oracle is DC Comics' superheroine, Batgirl. Having been shot through the spinal cord by the Joker, in her civilian identity, Batgirl became bound to a wheelchair. As a computer expert and information broker, she uses her skills and the codename Oracle to assist other superheroes, fighting crime.

If that's too much to remember, just think of me as Dopey, sweeping up the bounty from the floor of a diamond mine, positioned atop the historic Terminal Building across the river from downtown Pittsburgh.

Alex and the official Oracle of SteelGate Studio
(psst, that's me!)

23

Lab Monster

I f you've checked the price of prosthetics lately, you know they'll cost you an arm and a leg. Not having an arm or a leg is the reason I need them, but the cost is the primary reason I don't have any—ones that function, anyhow.

It's a catch twenty-two of a different proportion.

Sure, there has been a verity of limb-like gadgets—from the duck feet, to the banana arm and other such accessories, but none were completely and lastingly successful for my specific needs.

Counted individually, my prosthetic arms have totaled seventeen, which are probably more arms than what most people are known to have.

Among those, I include the ones Dad made from the little plastic football and drinking straws which allowed me to bat at my toys when I was an infant.

After that, it was on to the unsuccessful and completely non-functioning "monkey arms," which Mom told you about in *Unseen Arms*. I really don't remember those, and though I love monkeys, I'd rather forget them if I did.

My first prosthesis memory is of the single "banana arm" with the pincher hand, also mentioned in my first book. And I remember the spoon attachment, which was an accessory, not a prosthetic limb.

After the banana arm, I was fitted with a matching pair of arms with rubber hooks that served as "hands." Those worked fairly well for me, and I was actually able to paint my toenails with them.

Those arms came from Nemours/Alfred I. duPont Hospital for Children, in Wilmington, Delaware. When I outgrew them, I got another pair that was of the same configuration. That pair and most of my other prosthetics would be made by Union Artificial Limb & Brace because of the company's convenient Pittsburgh location, which saved us a three hundred mile drive to Wilmington, on the inner layer of the east coast.

My next fitting consisted of a pair of arms that had a hook on the right side and a passive hand on the left. The hook was my usable appendage, but the left hand was able to open and close a little.

The hand was also covered with a rubber flesh tone glove bearing imprints of fake nails on the fingertips. It wasn't the prettiest hand I'd ever seen, but considering that I'd never owned a hand, it really wasn't bad.

I liked the idea of having "fingernails" to paint, and I did paint them (with nail polish, not real paint). When going off to school in the wintertime, I would also tuck the hand into a white muff to keep it warm like the other girls did.

As time went on, my prosthetics improved in appearance. The last three pairs have consisted of matching arms and two hands with fleshy gloves that extend to the elbows.

I remember as a kid, when I got a "finger cut" somewhere on one of my rubber gloves, I had Mom place a bandage over it as if to offer a protective barrier for the wound. This made me feel that my appearance was more normal looking. But the overall aesthetic gain of having hands was a tradeoff for the loss of functionally, as limited as it had been.

By my sixth pair and beyond, my arms have been strictly passive. Essentially, they do two things: they drive my wheelchair, and they look good.

To mix things up a bit, the arms that I currently wear were made by Hanger Incorporated. They are known as the leading provider of prosthetics and orthotics throughout the world. They have also transcended beyond the human realm to the aquatic, as it was Hanger that designed and manufactured a prosthetic tail for Winter, a bottlenose dolphin who lost her tail after becoming entangled in a rope off the Florida coast. This remarkable feat inspired the 2011 movie *Dolphin Tale*.

Unlike Winter, I have learned to swim fine without a prosthetic tail, but should I ever need one, Hanger would be my likely choice for that. In the meantime, I'll just stick with the arms that they've made.

Like my preceding limbs, these current ones have no hand or joint movement. Therefore, when I drive, I'm completely unable to offer any appropriate hand signals. And I certainly wouldn't consider using the inappropriate ones.

As for looking good, there yet remains room for improvement with mine because the arms don't contain freckles like we part-time "redheads" are often known to have. There are professionally painted prosthetic gloves that can be customized with freckles, veins, even tattoos. But once again, insurance doesn't cover those features.

Mine look pretty decent, regardless.

When I was little, our annual jaunts to duPont were all about the hunt for prosthetics and whether or not we could find and afford some that would work for me.

We made those trips for three or four years, starting when I was five years old. That's the age when most kids are afraid of monsters, ogres, and other mythical creatures. Yet, there I was becoming one—a lab monster of sorts. That just sounds a little more like fun and a little less like work than being known as a test patient.

Beyond the search for prosthetic arms was the hunt for my basic independence. My time at duPont—during the week or so that we would be there—involved a healthy variety of experimentation in an attempt to reach that goal. With the use of various prosthetic arms, they had me picking things up, moving stuff around, and assembling matching pieces.

You know, general lab monster activities.

On one of our visits there, I also had my first experience with a powered wheelchair. Included among the arm exercises was an introductory driving lesson.

The chair wasn't the Turbo model that was shipped to us a short time later when I was maybe six years old. But I'm sure those test drives assisted my ability to operate mine so easily when it arrived.

In case you are wondering about the functional arms that I initially used when I was little, I discarded them after a few years. They were a simple body-powered design, and the muscle movements needed to operate them was very tiring on me.

Plus, I always hated the cables that went across my back. They were extremely uncomfortable, and every time I'd flex to open the hooks or relax to close them, the cables would pinch my skin. The end result was that I chose to go without. I made that decision when I was eight or nine, and our trips to Delaware then became a thing of the past.

It was many years later that Eric came into my life and founded *Arms Around Amy*. His perseverance brought it into existence. And a fundraising campaign began.

Primarily, this would involve publicity. Much of that came when Eric took it upon himself to contact *Pentecostal Evangel Magazine* which then ran a cover story on me in their August 2009 issue. I believe it was "National Limbless Appreciation Week," or "Disability Awareness Month."

Or something like that.

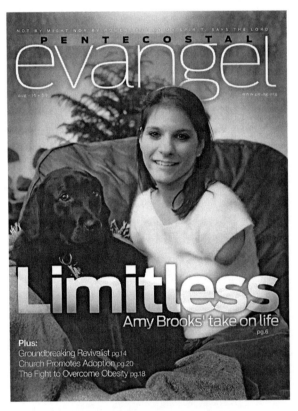

Cover of Pentecostal Evangel
August 2009

The exposure from the article eventually led me to sharing my testimony in book form. Twice.

My return to prosthesis window-shopping, as an adult, began with an assessment by Dr. Paul De La Torre to see if I was a viable candidate for myoelectric arms, which are what all the cool kids are wearing these days.

This design is very popular in prosthetic technology, and they greatly contrast the body-powered arms with the annoying straps and flesh-eating cables.

The myoelectric arms are custom-fitted to the user and normally attach only with suction, requiring no harnesses, straps, cables, buckles, or duct tape to hold them in position. This is another way that I'm different. My limbs are too short. I would require even more straps than my previous arms. Plus, the cast would extend into my chest.

Still, it seemed doable. Dr. Paul's team concluded that I was a candidate for the arms, but once they showed me the process and how they'd fit, I had reservations about them and concerns of being restricted.

This is an externally powered prosthesis, using a battery and electronic servos to function. With those components, I found the limbs to be quite heavy and bulky, and their movements were too slow for me.

Along the way, we all decided that the myoelectric arms were just not suitable for me. Nor were there currently any others that could perform the way that I needed them to.

Eventually, technological advancements will likely make the components of the myoelectric arms much lighter. Hopefully, they can also be made more affordable.

As it stands, the price tag is another very weighty part of them, and the funds that were raised to that point didn't come anywhere close to reaching the amount that we'd need for them. So, on my end, I continued to watch and wait for whatever else might come along.

Several years later, I crossed paths with a woman who was a fellow chiropractic patient with Dr. Green. After I left the office, she began questioning the doctors about me. It turned out that her brother-in-law was the head of the prosthetics department at the University of Pittsburgh.

The woman asked Dr. Green if he would contact me to see if I might consent to being a patient model for the students. Dr. Green agreed to ask me, and when he did, I agreed to participate.

And I've done it every fall semester since then.

Those lab duties are nothing overtly monstrous on my part; the prosthetics students do all the work. They simply borrow my upper extremities. With a team of two students on either side of me, they take turns casting my arms and using those molds to construct prosthetics with hooks and cables, just like the ones that I wore when I was younger.

During the first year, throughout the process, the students also worked together, trying to come up with things that would help me gain more independence. Though they always put forth a great amount of effort, we didn't really come up with any new solutions. I do appreciate their work, though. And they seem to appreciate me giving of my time to help them. I've also had so much fun that I remain in contact with some of those students.

My lab time there was and is time well spent.

Or well invested.

Though this is probably the only modeling career I'll ever have, it works well for me. Hopefully it will work well for others also. It's all part of the greater good for the benefit of future amputee patients. With each laboratory accomplishment, with every patient study or student experience comes the potential of improving the life of someone who stands in need of it.

From tests conducted and experiments performed to evaluations made and information shared, no scrap of knowledge goes to waste. Somewhere, somehow, I have to believe that it will eventually be applied, appropriately and effectively. That makes it all worth it.

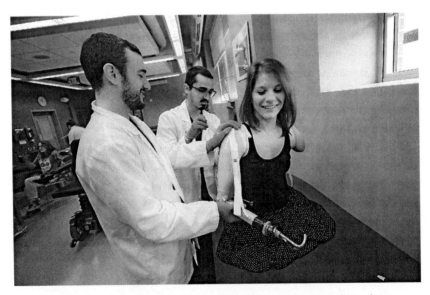

University of Pittsburgh Class of 2015 Prosthetics and Orthotics students learning to cast and fit prostheses

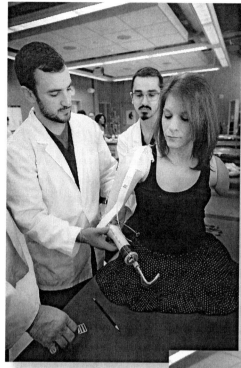

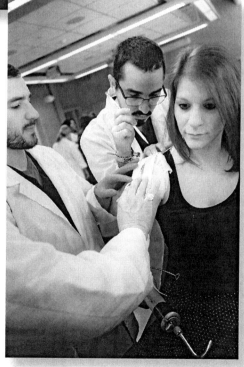

In *Unseen Arms*, I referenced the soldier who lost his legs in combat and then lost his life on a thrill ride. Allow me to reflect upon another whose story began more tragically, but had a triumphant ending, considering the circumstances.

This man suffered traumatic amputation of all four limbs in military combat. A few years later, he underwent a successful double-arm transplant from a deceased human donor. That technology and those capabilities are astounding. They give us causes to celebrate and reasons to hope.

Consider also a South African farmer who lost four fingers to a circular saw. The accident left him in constant pain and with permanent limitation. Plus, he couldn't afford the tens of thousands of dollars he'd need for a myoelectric hand.

"Sometimes you have to cut fingers off to start thinking," he said.

For $500.00, this man created a "Robohand" that allowed him to return to the carpentry profession. With donated funds, he also began making these hands for others worldwide, but he doesn't do it for profit.

He stated, "I don't want to make money out of misery."

There are also robotic hands that are now being created, which allows the wearer to feel the difference in sizes and shapes of various objects that they'd pick up. And these inventions are continually being tested and improved.

Look at 3-D printing and how it was used to create a plastic arm and hand for a seven-year-old California girl. And the cost was only $50.00!

Imagine future possibilities that await us through added research, through innovative practices, through continuing advancements. Every inch of it is necessary in formulating a better quality of life for amputees or for those who were born with physical challenges.

Certainly, we've come a long way, but great distances are yet to be traveled. Much time, effort, and a vast array of resources are required to create and deliver such developments.

For now, I'm okay with not being able to stick my elbow in my ear like everyone else can. But someday I'd like to conquer that.

As life goes on, so does my use of passive arms.

However, I continue to watch and wait and hope that, when something more suitable for me comes along, the funds will be there to purchase them.

The simple and unfortunate truth is that, regardless of what you may have learned of earth science, prosthetics technology says otherwise: limbs don't grow on trees.

24

Drops In the Bucket

I had already started without them, several years prior. It began with me bringing Eric to tears if you really want to count that. If so, it was only that one thing, a single meager act, an occurrence that didn't make the smallest of dents.

And being a lonely little drop in the bucket, neither did it create the slightest of splashes. But that status would change with a spot on the calendar marking the official launch in September 2014.

It was something that Eric spearheaded and had in the works—along with The Band of Brothers—for more than six months. There would be thrills to experience, challenges to embrace, and daring tasks to accomplish. This would be known collectively as "Amy's bucket list."

It's widely believed that we all have one—a catalog of things that we want to do or a list of places that we'd like to visit before our time comes to kick the bucket. If you have trouble finding yours, it's probably with your songwriting junkyard.

These lists can be printed as a hard copy or stored digitally with multiple backups. Some are likely to be greatly detailed. Others not as much.

Your list might be growing longer as you include additional wishes. Or, it could be getting shorter as you ambitiously fulfill those things and cross them off.

My bucket list is more of the ambiguous kind, invisible lines of non-specifics that were written only in my heart.

The vagueness of my list signifies my approach to it all. There have always been things that I'd like to try, but I wouldn't care what those activities would be, generally speaking.

I think I'd just nod my head to about anything audacious.

It wouldn't matter if I had a chance to scuba dive or jump from an airplane. You could shoot me out of a cannon for all I cared. I'd simply like to get out and experience some unique adventures.

That's what Eric had been working on, and the time had finally arrived where we'd get everything underway, carrying out those activities. It all began on the very weekend of my birthday. And the gifts were unbelievably generous from the start.

Amy Knievel

Most of you have at least heard of him, a man with whom I am now fashionably connected by way of a rumbling two-wheel mechanical invention known as a motorcycle. "Kaptain" Robbie Knievel: professional daredevil and motorcycle stuntman.

Minus the takeoff ramp and a long deadly expanse, my first outing would involve me and a Harley-Davidson. The plan was to place me in a sidecar and thunder down the highway at the posted speed limit.

Or, maybe a little over if we don't tell Mom.

Being dedicated Harley guys, it was of no shock that the collaborative thinking of Eric and The Brothers would include that specific and spectacular machine and that type of activity for me.

To achieve a convincing biker chick look, I had chosen to wear my black faux leather jacket, which nicely complimented my black spaghetti strap dress and black and white polka dot sunglasses.

Topping things off, literally, a Brother named Fernando—who was also a fellow high school graduate of mine—offered me the use of his helmet.

I had the look down, but before the ride, Eric took me birthday shopping in the store, Gatto's Cycle Shop, in Tarentum. The girls who worked there were so very accommodating of Logic and me. Gladly, they assisted us as we looked around and made our selections. I picked out a black Harley tank top, which I would save to wear the next day for my other planned events.

Though Logic would not be actually riding with us, she chose a nice bandana for herself, bearing a swirl of orange flames and the famous Harley logo. Of course, she was already wearing black by nature. This allowed her to look the part as she hung out at the shop. We tried the bandana on Logic a few different ways, and the girls took pictures of her to post on the store's webpage.

With that, we were "all systems go."

Under clear, sunny skies of perfect weather, my ride would begin with a little test run—much like what Kaptain Knievel might do to try things out, I suppose.

Eric lifted me into the sidecar, placed a pillow behind my back, and helped me get comfortably situated in the bucket seat. Being my first time inside such a machine, I found it to have plenty of legroom, thank you.

On the rare occasions that I'm relegated to using my non-powered wheelchair for conveyance, I use a Velcro-connecting stretchy belt around my waistline to hold me in it because the chair came with a standard lap belt—and I didn't come with a standard lap. My parents brought the belt to the Harley shop, and we used it to bind me to the bucket seat of the sidecar.

Besides Eric, a handful of Brothers were in attendance and would participate in the ride on their own bikes. There was also Eric's friend, Tony, who wasn't part of The Band of Brothers, and Tim who would be videotaping everything.

We also had a lead vehicle, a pickup truck, driven by James. Tim would collect his video footage while riding from a standing position in the back of the pickup. Shop owner Mark Gatto would pilot the motorcycle carrying the sidecar and me.

Before heading out, Mom and Dad inspected my ride conditions. As usual, Dad didn't say much. But Mom voiced some concern that I might somehow come flying out of it. She made it clear that she'd put a serious hurt on Eric if anything happened to me.

He assured her with his life that nothing would happen. And it would probably cost him that with Mom if something did.

Our test run was a slow spin around the block to see if I felt safe and if anything needed adjusted before hitting the main roads. Everything went smoothly, and I felt completely secure.

My parents and everyone then gathered around as Eric asked a blessing over my first-ever Harley ride.

"Keep the bugs out of her teeth, keep the wind in her hair," he prayed, in typical biker form.

And then, we were off.

I had become a little sweaty waiting in the black jacket beneath the helmet and glaring sun. When we started moving, the airflow was much invited and extremely refreshing.

Initially, we stayed on winding country roads. I felt so close to the trees going by. And I could see everything!

In my wheelchair, inside our van, my vision is greatly restricted because my ride height places me above the window line. Typically, I have only an obstructed view through the windshield.

By leaning forward, I can see a little out the side window as well. But that's about it. So, when riding, my viewing choices have mostly been limited to two selections:

A) *Look at the back of Dad's head.*

B) *Look at the back of Mom's head.*

Neither of which are very appealing by the way.

But don't tell them I said that.

Out there on the road, in that sidecar, it was a different story. I could fully enjoy the mountains from the ground to the sky. I drank in the fresh air and soaked up the many intricate sights of Pittsburgh's beautifully patented topography.

With Eric and the others riding along—sometimes in front of Mark and me, sometimes behind—my ride came to resemble a presidential motorcade or some type of high profile escort.

Mom had worried that I wouldn't be secure, but I had to brace myself a lot less in the sidecar than I do when riding in our van. So, I was able to just relax, let Mark do the driving, and take everything in.

After a while, Mark asked if I wanted to go on the highway or stick to the winding roads. I asked what he preferred. He said the winding roads let you feel the bike a little more, but the highway would bring more speed. I voted for the speed.

Mark gunned the throttle, and we hit highway.

Blazing along a foot or so above the pavement was an incredible experience. The speed, the low-end rumble, the brain-rattling vibration—it was all so new and invigorating. Much more so than riding my walker down the wheelchair ramp when I was a kid.

In all, we rode for about an hour or so. Our highway speed hovered around seventy, a pace that seems much faster being in the open air and so close to ground.

I could truly see why bikers love riding as they do.

My motorcycle experience might not have mirrored the Kaptain's highly celebrated 170-foot-long fountain jump at Caesar's Palace, which avenged the disastrous attempt by his famous father, forever known as "Evel" Knievel.

But to me it was just as thrilling.

Thankfully, Tim recorded every inch of it without tumbling from the back of the pickup truck. And Mark said I'm welcome to come back and ride again, any time I'd like!

Amy Knievel with Mark Gatto

Biker gang

Amy Oakley

Some things are just too dramatic to forget. I had just fulfilled a speaking engagement at Valley Gospel Church, on September 14, when—two weeks prior to my bucket list kickoff—two men approached me, wielding a rifle.

They placed the gun near my face and held it there. They then began to question me. I believe it may have qualified as a full-on interrogation session. These guys wanted answers. They were requesting information that only I could provide.

Yet, I couldn't, really.

But I was confident I would be able to identify these dudes in a police lineup if necessary. One I knew quite well. These armed individuals were widely known as Eric Fabian and his friend, John Fulmer. They claimed to be testing my sight, which proved to be a nerve-racking experience.

With the butt of the empty rifle resting against my shoulder and the barrel aimed outward, they wanted to know how I could handle the thing well enough to shoot it. And it would all begin with my vision.

Unlike my bothersome, mismatched hip sockets and the two-inch variance in my arm lengths, my eyes are identical. As far as I know, they were issued and installed as a matching set. Both are the same in size, shape, and color, and they are positioned in proper alignment and spaced the appropriate distance. They are also sufficiently accessorized with corresponding lashes and brows. (The mascara and eyeliner came later, at my choosing.)

Additionally, these eyes have always gotten along well with one another. So, I had no idea which of the two was considered dominant. Making that determination was a muddled and convoluted task.

Until that moment, the topic just never came up. It wasn't part of everyday conversation. Eye dominance was something that I hadn't really thought about. Suddenly, I was forced to do so, in the presence of a deadly weapon. And I was clueless as to what these guys were truly asking.

"When you focus on my finger," said Eric, "close one eye, and then switch to the other. At which time does my finger move?"

And things like that.

He might as well have been speaking military code or space alien talk. I had no idea. I couldn't tell. My vision in each eye seemed to be the same, as did Eric's fingers and hairy knuckles. Nothing appeared to move at all. Nothing changed.

Was it just me, or what?

Somehow, we either guessed or concluded that I was right-eye dominant...probably. So, we eventually went with that. As difficult as it was to arrive at this conclusion, John had been handed a much harder assignment. But Eric was confident that if anyone was capable of carrying out the work, it was John Fulmer.

John is an intelligent and talented guy with a degree in metallurgy. He is a research machinist and full-time college professor, who teaches a manufacturing course in the engineering department at Pittsburgh's Carnegie Mellon University. John also has a long, solid background in the diversified methods of welding, soldering, and brazing.

With this wide range of knowledge and impressive skill set, Eric figured the project would simply be another day at work for John. But it would turn out to be anything but simple.

Between my two seemingly matching eyes, I would have to puncture a bright red one on an imaginary bull made of thin flat cardboard at a firing range.

To accomplish this, Eric had asked John, a few months earlier, to design and build some sort of contraption to connect to my wheelchair that would allow me to shoot a gun—particularly a .22 semiautomatic rifle, since it doesn't have much kick when fired. This would be my second bucket list event, the day after the Harley ride.

After giving it great consideration, John decided he couldn't really do much without seeing me and my chair to assess what my abilities were and what he'd have to work with.

It was coming down to the wire. So, after my speech at Valley Gospel, Eric, Miss Heidi, their son, Jesse, my parents, and Logic and I converged on John's house.

He really needed me there. So there I was, with the butt of the rifle planted against my shoulder and my cheek resting on the gunstock.

We were all outside on a large concrete approach that led into the garage. That's where the brainstorming began. Jesse's job was to entertain Logic who kept getting in between John and me, vying for attention. The rest of us went to work on how to come up with something to turn me into a qualified marksman.

Right-eye dominant had been agreed upon, but squeezing the trigger would be the hardest part. How would I shoot? Was I right-armed or a lefty? This is another distinction that I'm continually faced with, especially when trying something new.

Apparently, a person without hands is capable of bearing the unique label of ambidextrous. For some tasks, I predominantly use my right arm. For others, I favor my left. It all depends on what I'm doing.

Having never been through sniper training, I didn't know which arm would be better for handling semiautomatic weaponry or how to fire a shot.

My "trigger arm" kept changing with every idea. At one time it was the left arm, and then the right, and back to the left.

Who knows?

John also had to consider things that others likely take for granted, such as how well I'd be able to balance and steady myself. Among the tasks would be adjusting the gun to a proper height for me to see down the sight.

With John taking measurements and making notes and sketches, he and Eric and Dad discussed everything in detail. The more I studied the gun and played with it, the more I understood how I might successfully control it. I then began offering suggestions of my own.

The guys had been contemplating multiple arms for me to completely hold the gun and the use of strings to pull the trigger. I was thinking more simply. (Sometimes, less is more.) It would be better to mount it, independently, and figure out how I could aim and fire it.

By the end of the meeting, John had some workable ideas. But time was of the essence. The clock was ticking, loudly. From there, I went on to my other obligations, and John set out to work an engineering miracle, in twelve days or less.

On September 25th—the day before my bucket list activities were to officially begin—Eric and Miss Heidi invited my parents and me to dinner at their place. Several other guests were there, including John Fulmer.

Turns out, the gathering was in celebration of my birthday, along with a few others whose birthdays were around the same time as mine. By the end of the night, John and I discovered that we shared the same birthday—September 28th.

John had brought along the rifle adaptation that he had been working on. So, we also used the night to discuss last-minute modifications for it.

What John had come up with was quite impressive, proving that he was the right man for the job. Everything was adjustable to accommodate for varied height choices and body positioning. But we still hadn't figured out how I could activate the trigger. Everyone was out there offering ideas, but by the end of the night, I didn't think we had much to go on.

The next morning was the Harley ride, and the day after would be the shooting range. This didn't leave John much time to figure it out, and none of us would know what he'd have until the time came for me to use it.

On that morning, my parents, Eric, Jesse, and I headed out to the Millvale Sportsmen's Club in nearby Wexford. Of course, Logic was there also, and Tim arrived to do the video recording.

Being the giving person that he is, John was off helping someone in his neighborhood with a home project that they were having trouble with. They had asked him to swing by and offer an opinion. This meant he wouldn't be at the firing range to observe his innovation in action. So, Dad and Eric set it up for me.

Tim manned the camera.

Jesse set up my target.

The rifle was center mounted on a gun stand that connected to the front of my wheelchair, which was great. But I immediately noticed that I wasn't able to freely aim because there was no movement to it. John had added a second mounting bracket that secured the butt of the gun to the back of my seat.

That was the only part of the design that I didn't like. What was the point in shooting if all I would do was pull the trigger? Doesn't the fun and challenge come from seeing how well you can aim? This being the case, I asked Eric to remove the additional piece and let me place the butt against my shoulder where it belonged.

Much better!

The gun's movement could now be controlled at the pivot point of the mount. I would aim and fire from my right shoulder, actuating the trigger with my left arm.

The trigger adaptation was ingenious.

Inside the trigger case was a cam that John had made of Lexan—a lightweight polycarbonate plastic material that wouldn't scratch or mar the gunmetal.

He used a setscrew to attach the cam to a metal rod that crossed in front of me, from the trigger case to my left shoulder. Clamped to the rod was a flat wooden paddle.

When ready to fire, I would do so by pressing down on the paddle with the endpoint of my left arm. The paddle would roll the rod, which would move the cam. The cam would then push the trigger straight back. After each shot, I would then push the paddle up to let the cam rotate forward, allowing the trigger to reset.

Simple, right?

With that, I had twenty rounds.

To visually gage how much kick the gun would have, I asked Eric to test fire the first shot, which he did on a separate lane. I observed no mechanical recoil, whatsoever.

Eric then briefed me on how to aim and instructed me to stay as still as possible while pulling the trigger. For my first shot, he would hold his hand underneath the gun, so I could maintain control and just get the feel of it.

I steadied myself and aimed with the eye that had been voted most dominant. A rush of adrenaline washed over me. Through my hearing protection came the sound of my pounding heartbeat.

Slowly, I pushed down on the paddle, and…

…nothing happened.

I hadn't set the trigger by pushing the paddle up far enough.

So, I reset and tried again.

Pop!

At first, I couldn't see where I had shot and could only hold my breath and hope I had at least hit the target. I did! It was in the eight range! Not bad.

From there, Eric let go and turned me loose. I reset the trigger and took a deep breath. Concentrated…steadied…aimed.

Pop!

Shot number two was in the nine range, but I knew I could do better.

Pop!

Shot number three was just inside the red. Bull's-eye!

What! That had to have been an accident. Jesse must have pushed the target in front of my bullet, right? Or, was there a second shooter somewhere? Was Eric firing a service weapon over my shoulder?

Nope, it was all me!

Repeating the process, I squeezed them off, one after another.

Pop…pop…pop…and more pops.

Nineteen live rounds.

When it was all over—when the dust settled and the smoke cleared—I have to admit, I was thoroughly impressed with my shooting and had to have a couple of photos taken of me with my target.

The pictures don't lie; there was nothing on the outer two rows of the target—no sevens or sixes.

Ten of my shots were in the ten range.

Six were in the nine.

Three were in the eight.

And there were no dead birds or downed aircraft on my account!

A modern day Annie Oakley, perhaps? Her legendary sharpshooting abilities earned her the nickname, "Little Sure Shot." I can live with that—as sort of a metric equivalent.

At least the "little" part fits me exceptionally well.

With Dad being former military and Eric a cop, I'm hoping one of them might see fit to nominate me for an official marksmanship award!

If nothing else, at least I made them smile.

Them and me both.

Amy Oakley

"Yabba Dabba Doo!"

Upon leaving the shooting range, we immediately headed for the home of Dale and Karen Biernesser—good people who are close friends with Eric. Dale is a Brother, and Miss Karen used to teach my mid-week *Bible* class at our church when I was a kid.

If you punch their home address into your navigational system, it will lead you to two beautiful acres of privately-owned land that is geographical located fifteen miles true north of Pittsburgh, to an area that's typically known by the locals as Gibsonia, Pennsylvania.

The Biernesser's likely aren't aware of it, but their property is actually a remaining piece from the Flintstones' town of Bedrock. That's not to say the place is old, but...well...okay, I suppose the ground that it sets on is old, but the Flintstones connotation emanates from the activity that would occur there for my next bucket list event.

There, on the Biernesser property, I would be driving a slightly modified Bimmer, which is the proper accepted slang for Bedrock mobiles (not to be confused with a Beemer, which is the motorcycle version by the same primitive manufacturer).

Most bystanders would view this Bimmer, this Bedrock mobile, as an ordinary golf cart. And you may think of it as such because that's what was used in the making of the actual Flintstones movies that involved real human actors. Decorated golf carts became convincing physical replicas of the cartoon version of that fictitious prehistoric vehicle, and that's what I'd be driving on that day.

It was the deluxe package, the *500 Series* of all Flintstone cars, one that didn't have to be peddled with bare feet.

In addition to the use of their land, the Biernesser's provided the golf cart for me to perform my driving endeavor. And Eric had brought along a couple of items that no one should ever leave home without—metal bicycle handlebars, which he and Dale were prepared to modify by bending, cutting, or whatever it took to supply me with a useable method of steering and an aluminum crutch for whoever's foot I'd run over.

As Logic ran off to explore the land and Tim worked his video camera, I sat on the seat of the golf cart. Similar to working with the rifle at John's house, we quickly formed an engineering committee. It was Dale, Eric, Dad, and me mulling things over. Collectively, we swirled so many ideas around and did enough brainstorming to have created a tornado over the area.

After discussing some ideas, Dale and Eric would then disappear into the garage like a couple of elves into Santa's toyshop. But this was a toyshop for big boys, not elves. The place quickly erupted with flames and sparks and the sound of various industrial noises.

The guys made several trips back and forth. I waited in the driver's seat like a racecar driver on pit road. Each time they returned, the four of us continued to brainstorm. Dale and Eric had begun the modifications by using a cutoff wheel to remove the right half of the handlebars to clear it out of the way. They also lit up an oxy-acetylene torch to heat the metal, so the handlebar could be bent back a little more within my reach.

Thankfully, they were kind enough to quench the thing with water before allowing me to touch it.

Eventually, they also constructed a strap clamp from a piece of sheet metal, drilled a hole through it, and managed to wrap it over the center of the steering column and fasten it with a bolt. This allowed me to control the steering wheel by bringing it further toward me, where I'd use my left arm to turn it.

The crutch was actually brought along as a suggestion from Jesse; he thought of me using it to reach the gas pedal, which was genius…with a *G*. Not like the Amy kind with a *J*.

After adjusting the crutch to the suitable length, the guys used duct tape to secure the end of it to the gas pedal. I would control that from my right arm.

Having forgotten to bring my stretchy Velcro belt with us, Eric wrapped several passes of duct tape around me and the seat.

"With God and duct tape, all things are possible," I joked.

Only half true, of course, but we had a good laugh about it.

Dale sat next to me on the golf cart. He would be my crash test dummy if something unfavorable were to happen.

Before we started, he briefed me on how to turn the wheel, when to apply the gas, and when to let up. There was one particular hill on the property where he said to lift off the gas, completely, going downhill, and the cart would roll by itself. He would apply the brake pedal when necessary and also help steer if I lost hold of the handlebar.

Got it!

With Fernando's motorcycle helmet again strapped firmly on my head, we were off. You'd think if I held it under seventy and kept at least two wheels on the ground at all times, I'd do fine.

Let's not overcomplicate it. It's driving. The State of Pennsylvania graciously issued a valid driver's license to Mom and Dad. How hard can it be?

Turned out to be tougher than I expected.

Patches of rough terrain made it difficult, and the whole driving experience took a lot of getting used to. There were areas where I handled it well on my own, but if I'd hit the gas too hard, the rapid acceleration would shove me back in the seat where I couldn't reach to steer.

So, Dale assisted.

When going on a slight downgrade, gravity would lean me closer to the wheel, and I could reach again.

After a couple of times around the property, I started to get the hang of it. At that point it became a Saturday afternoon drive. God's sunlight shone down upon us. Birds cheered me on with their lively chirps. And seeing Amy at the controls, squirrels and crickets all scampered for their dear little lives.

It was practically a scene from *Driving Miss Daisy.*

Except it was Miss Daisy who was doing the driving.

Fortunately, unlike Hoke Colburn—Morgan Freeman's character in the film—Dale didn't have to stop to "go make water" along the way.

Next in was Eric. With him onboard, the Miss Daisy experience quickly vanished, replaced by Stone Age intelligence.

We started out like Fred and Barney, good buddies, close pals, partners through thick and thin...and through commercial breaks for sugary breakfast cereals.

Eric was Fred Flintstone—the loud, obnoxious, take-charge guy in the crowd. I was Barney Rubble—much smaller, quieter, and compliant. Barney is also the smart one, a theory that was soon to be proven.

Be assured, I remained diligent at fulfilling my assigned responsibilities. Pushing against the crutch, I accelerated at the appropriate time and lifted when I needed to. And I kept up with my steering enough to avoid all human spectators, natural wildlife, and manmade structures in the area.

Eric had one simple task to perform, and he tanked it. The incident occurred as we crested the one particular hill that had a significant down slope. I lifted off the gas as I had done when *Driving Miss Dale* or whatever.

But this time, with Eric, I experienced complete brake failure and went blazing down the hill, at NASCAR speeds. Just when I thought Danica Patrick would have been proud, I lost all control of the steering, the whole way down, and fearfully resorted to my multitasking abilities:

outwardly, I was screaming like a girl, inwardly, I was praying to high heaven that the duct tape would hold me in the seat.

Had there been a rollover accident and an ensuing crash scene investigation, the findings would have conclusively shown that the only true brake failure was in Eric's failure to use them.

In retrospect, it probably wasn't much different than Fred Flintstone sliding down the tail of a dinosaur at the end of his workday. The only missing ingredient was that I didn't hear Eric hollering, "Yabba dabba doo!"

Then again, that might have been merely covered over by the far-reaching decibels of my own girlish screams.

Despite the outcome, that brakeless, reckless ordeal was very scary. It was terrifying…and also a bit exhilarating.

But it was dangerous of Eric to not apply the brakes.

On the other hand, it was kind of cool to have survived it so I can write about it in my book.

In the end, "terrifying" won out. Eric's trip was over after that one pass around the property. Before the ride had even come to a safe and complete stop, I ordered him out of the golf cart. If there was someplace he needed to be, he could thumb it for all I cared. I just knew he wouldn't be riding with me any further.

For the most part, the golf cart driving was fun. I appreciated all the work that the guys had put forth, but it was extremely challenging and not something I think I'd want to do more of.

Danica has nothing to worry about; I probably don't have much a future in NASCAR racing.

Jesse was a different story, though. He had been bouncing off his rambunctious energy on the Biernesser's trampoline, waiting for me to be done driving so he could carjack the golf cart. He then drove it all over the property, around and around and back and forth, using any excuse he could think of to get more wheel time.

Dale and Miss Karen invited us all to stay and eat and to make s'mores desserts around a campfire. Of course, Jesse offered to chauffeur my dad from the front of the property to the back where the campfire would be.

It was my first-ever campfire experience, and I loved it.

In contrast to trying to kill me on the golf cart, Eric made sure that I was completely comfortable sitting on the ground, giving me a little cushion to sit on and a tree log to lean against.

We had pizza and hotdogs for dinner, and it was the perfect ending to a very busy, crazy, unforgettable couple of days and an amazing way to bring in my birthday.

Logic enjoyed it as much as any of us; she ran the entire property like a maniac and then wandered around to sniff everything. Eric roasted some hotdogs for her. With that, she was in doggie heaven.

Regarding heaven, in general, only God knows what else might have come my way concerning these bucket list events. During their scheming and planning sessions, one of the Brothers, James, a firefighter, had suggested, "Let's take her to the firehouse, put up the tall aerial ladder, throw her in a backpack, and carry her to the top of the ladder."

When Eric asked how many feet high that would be, James casually replied, "Only a hundred and ten."

That event didn't happen.

Knowing how Mom would be about it, Eric immediately dismissed the idea. He flatly stated, "Janet would never allow it."

And he was right, I'm sure.

He said Mom would have torn them in half.

Maybe I didn't give him enough credit. Eric might actually be a tad bit smarter than Fred Flintstone, after all.

Yabba Dabba Doo!

"Full Pull!"

Some things are planned, as those specific activities were. Other things just happen. Both can be rewarding and enjoyable, depending on the experience or circumstance, of course.

Some people may hold long anticipation for a special occurrence, such as a vacation, family gathering, or celebration. They watch for its arrival, check the days off the calendar, and wait, eagerly. It could be that you are someone who'd want things that way—completely expected, nothing unprompted or spur-of-the-moment.

Others might prefer the element of surprise, not knowing what lies around the next bend, having that unforeseen fragment of spontaneity dart out, seemingly, from nowhere. Maybe that would be your personal preference.

You just never know what can happen or how your wishes might be fulfilled from one day to the next or from one situation to the next. Maybe Brett Barry will stop by your home, someday, to eat a plate of homemade lasagna. If he does, and if he's packing a guitar, he'll probably even play you a song or two.

Myself, I've always been flexible. When it comes to getting ready to go somewhere, I definitely like to prepare. But after I'm out of the house, I'm pretty much open for whatever comes along. Planning and preparedness are greatly beneficial, but I've certainly experienced a fair amount of surprises as well.

Concerning my actual private, unwritten bucket list, one thing that was on it for many years was something quite basic, but it had not been fulfilled: I've always wanted to go out onto a beach.

Any beach, anywhere, at any time.

I knew they existed. I had seen them in Florida. But I had never been on one. I often wanted to know what it was like to leave my tracks in its surface and feel the warm grains of sand beneath my bare wheels.

Noah was lucky enough to go to the beach in Erie, Pennsylvania, in late July 2014. He and Theresa had taken the kids there on a daytrip for a family getaway.

Unfortunately, that luck ran out with Noah losing his keys somewhere, presumably, in the sand. And there was no finding them.

It would be a drive of only 125 miles or so, one way, to deliver a spare car key to them. However, I have a feeling Dad might not appreciate reading the word "only" in that sentence. I can imagine him reaching for a pen to cross it out because he would be the one making that drive.

But for me, it became an opportunity.

Road Trip for Amy! I call shotgun!

Or, maybe I'll just ride in the back.

I'm living proof that life is made from a recipe that is as impracticable as it is unpredictable. I had no idea that I might fulfill a bucket list wish that day; I just wanted to go along and at least see the Lake Erie shoreline.

But that mindset changed once we got there. Rolling out of the van, I decided I would not settle for being this close to a beach again without sampling the beautiful sandy terrain. The car key handoff was a great diversion, providing cover for me to make a break for it.

Thanks, Noah!

The only thing that lay before me was a few trees and a berm of earth that likely served to prevent flooding and beach erosion. I revved my engine, expectantly. And then, I did as a comedian named Mike Warnke once said; "I put it in 'B' for Boogie."

Full throttle.

No hesitation.

No looking back.

After traveling the distance of maybe a hundred feet, I arrived at my intended destination. Within seconds of cresting the hill, I struck beach as I had so desired!

It was then that I discovered everything that I had heard of beaches to be completely true, how their physical characteristics of loose, dry sand is not prominently conducive to a heavy, slow-rolling motorized wheelchair driven by…well…*me!*

That is to say I encountered a beige-colored bog consisting of innumerable granulates that would grind me to an abrupt halt. My only progress at that point was in the burying of my wheelchair nearly to its axles.

Having always had my back, Noah came to my immediate rescue as he had done so many times, in so many ways, when we were kids. On this day, a good full push would be needed to get me rolling again.

Said Noah of the incident:

"I had to crouch down low to pick the backend of the wheelchair up and push forward at the same time, so the front drive wheels would get traction. I felt like a football player pushing one of those tackling sleds the length of the football field. I was sweaty and out of breath with my legs burning from the lactic acid build-up after a good workout, but it was all worth it to see the look on Amy's face. And after all, it was the least I could do; they did just drive 250 miles, round trip, for me. I was relishing the moment until the thought went through my head, *Oh no, I have to push her off the beach!* Well, time to suit up and hit the tackling sled again!"

First, Noah loses his car keys, and then he finds himself pushing his silly sister out of the sand. It was like adding in salt to an injury that's a wound.

Or however that goes.

I probably could have at least offered to search for his missing keys for him, but that didn't happen.

I did appreciate the push, though.

It seemed if my wheelchair only had more power, more torque, more ponies under the hood—if that "B" gear had fully engaged—I could have freed myself from the sandy bog and boogied across the beach. Maybe my ride would be quicker if it weren't trimmed in girlish purple. That's the way it all seemed at the time.

An unexpected event that happened two months later offered an appearance that was much different: one in great contrast to the notion that my chair was lacking power, and one that had a more favorable outcome. This unscheduled occurrence would unfold as another bucket list rendering of its own. It happened when I encountered a nightmare on a wet but sunny Saturday afternoon on the date of October 5, 2014.

It was the weekend after my official bucket list outing, and the perfect weather that had graced us six days earlier had now taken flight, overthrown by its evil nemesis.

The gathering was for the annual *Unity in the Community*, billed as a "free picnic and festival of hope." It was held at Etna Ball Field, in Pittsburgh, and was badly hampered by an overabundance of ambient cold and sideways rain. I was invited to speak there on that day, but everything was off schedule because of the weather.

Several of my family members were there in an act of support and to help out. Besides my parents, there was Jodi and Candy. Also Noah and Theresa and the kids, Ben and Grace, were there. We were outside for hours. My merch table was set up under a tent to display my books and artwork. At one point, a storm blew in so boisterously that it nearly snatched the tent away.

Concerning atmospheric conditions and its interaction with humankind, it was Mark Twain who said, "Everybody talks about the weather, but nobody does anything about it."

Obviously, he never met my family.

They were doing *everything* about it.

In a choreographed team effort, each of them sprang into action to avoid a disaster. Theresa and Grace began flipping my pictures over on the table and covering them to protect them from rain damage. Dad, Candy, Noah, and Ben each held onto a pole, so the tent wouldn't disappear into the menacing clouds like Dorothy's house in the tornado seen in *Wizard Of Oz*.

I pretty much just sat there and watched, shivering in the dampness.

But eventually, around midafternoon, the weather cleared, and the sun decided to drop in on us. And unlike Dorothy and Toto, Logic and I remained solidly in Pittsburgh. After a lengthy weather delay, a Christian music group took the stage. I would speak after them.

While sitting at my table and waiting for my adjusted timeslot to arrive, I began eyeing up a white monster truck that was parked across the field.

It was an attention-grabbing piece of machinery. Though we have all at least seen pictures and television footage of these massive contraptions, I had never physically seen one roaming in the wild or resting in its natural habitat. As I observed the magnificence of the sun sparkling off the smooth, glossy monster, someone suggested that I get my picture taken in front of it.

Though it had never been on my bucket list, I felt a spontaneous wish developing within me. Quietly, I confided to Candy, "I'd like to get in it."

Of course, there was no way I'd ever ask someone to lift me into a monster truck, especially one that was owned by some stranger. I felt I'd be imposing to even have my picture taken by it. So, I opted to simply enjoy looking at the thing. It was an impressive piece of mechanical art. And the name of the truck, in sky-blue lettering, was intriguing: *Daddy's Nightmare*.

As the band neared the completion of their set list, an event organizer brought a guy over to introduce to me. His name was Bob Grill, and he was the owner of the monster truck. When Bob kindly and unexpectedly offered to take me over to check out the truck, Candy piped up and said, "She wants to get in the thing!"

(That's the last time I share my thoughts with her, right?)

Bob said he'd be glad to let me do that, but he also had another idea; he wanted to set up a special photo op for me. This would involve him hooking a tow strap to the back of my wheelchair and to the back of his truck. He said it would appear as if my little wheelchair was pulling his huge truck, and it would make a great picture.

And then, it was Mom's turn to pipe up. She asked why we couldn't also put things in motion and get a video of it.

So, Bob hooked us up and told me to drive forward until I felt tension on the strap. Logic would be "helping." Her leash was hooked to the font of my chair, so she could offer some additional pulling muscle. Bob was concerned that she might freak out over the sound of the truck starting, but I assured him she'd be okay.

With that, he climbed into the truck and fired the engine.

As I drove forward, he backed up slowly. All the while, Bob was gunning the truck's engine to create the illusion that he was pulling against me.

I worked the chair pretty hard. And since it had been raining, I was spinning my wheels, digging up the mud, and throwing wet sod behind me. Of course, this made it look all the more convincing that I was out-pulling the truck.

Plus, we never lost tension on the strap.

Logic certainly did her part. She was pulling for all she was worth, and I coached her through the entire pull. "C'mon, Lolly, are we pulling? Keep going!" She was so excited and really cute; she thought she was actually helping to accomplish some monumental task.

Pull, Lolly!

It was fun and made a great video.

My only serious concern was for the band that was playing. We were only about 150 feet from the stage, and the truck was extremely loud. Though the actual pull only lasted a little over a minute, I felt that I gypped them of their stage time or at least ruined an otherwise good song. They had already been rumbled out by an autumn thunderstorm, and now they were being rumbled out by an Amy.

Well, it was *Daddy's Nightmare* that was doing the rumbling. I suppose we can blame that on Bob Grill.

On the other hand, it might have seemed appropriate if the band had stopped, mid-song, and the singer yelled, "Full pull!" into the microphone.

After all, I did out-pull a monster truck!

When it was over and we cut our engines, Bob and Noah lifted me into the driver's seat to have my picture taken through the open door. For Noah, it seemed much easier lifting me into the truck than pushing me out of the sand in Erie.

And though this side event—this "nightmarish" encounter—was not planned, designed, or predicted, it undoubtedly became a bonus drop in my proverbial bucket list.

Directly after the impromptu photo shoot, I headed straight to the stage to tell my story. Bob wanted to stay and listen but said he was scheduled to take his truck to a church for *Touch A Truck*, an event where kids could get their picture taken with it.

He was already running a little late and had to get *Daddy's Nightmare* loaded on the trailer and ready to go. But just as he had finished and was about to head out, Bob heard me, over the PA system, saying a closing prayer at the end of my presentation. With that, he couldn't help but to come back and buy a book and have me sign it before I had a chance to leave the stage.

I would learn the next day that the church Bob was headed to was my church, Allison Park! Turns out, Bob is friends with one of our pastors, Gregg Jacobs. Bob had no idea that I attend Allison Park, nor did I know that Bob was headed there.

I was aware that we were having a *Touch A Truck* event at our church that day, but having never been much of a mathematician, I just never put two and two together.

(If I had used the Common Core system, it wouldn't have been difficult; two and two can be anything you want it to be.)

Sharing my testimony at Unity in the Community in 2014

Still, it was Pastor Gregg who clued me in. He said Bob arrived with his truck and was telling him about having just met a woman in a wheelchair who had no arms and no legs and was sharing her testimony at *Unity in the Community.*

Apparently, Pastor Gregg is much better at math than I am—Common Core or otherwise—because he immediately realized Bob was speaking about me.

In the end, the bucket list activities were exciting, including the bonus encounter with *Daddy's Nightmare.* But there are bigger, more meaningful things that I'd like to conquer—things that would help me toward gaining more independence. With possible in-home adaptations, I'd like to learn to cook and simply take better care of myself, autonomously.

I'd also love to drive, someday. Not wheelchair drive, real drive. It might sound picky, but I'd like it to be something bigger than the Flintstone mobile, but smaller than *Daddy's Nightmare*.

In the meantime, I might contemplate starting a towing service. With Logic's help and a good tow strap, I believe I can make a go of it. The bulk of my confidence rests in my brother. Should I ever find myself in too deep, Noah will be there to give me a good push.

25

Retooling

Though we often may wish otherwise, life isn't all fun and games and the fulfilling of bucket list activities and other such adventures. Sometimes, additional situations come along that are equally as necessary. General upkeep and overdue repairs are frequently needed with things along the way.

Dad has always been a fixer. My male relatives own a collection of tools. Eric is a mechanical guy, as are John Fulmer and Dale Biernesser, obviously.

Depending on their quality, how often they are used, and how well they are maintained, tools will eventually have to be serviced or replaced. A saw will require a new blade. Drill bits have to be sharpened. That missing screwdriver or broken ratchet wrench will need to be repurchased.

The same is true of my personal tools, and not just the art utensils or computer equipment. This involves my own natural, God-given tools—the ones that I probably use more than most people while accomplishing my everyday tasks. These tools are my teeth and gums. All of which are usually led around by my face.

Whether or not one might consider my face a tool is yet to be officially determined. My chin certainly is. It can also be declared a deadly weapon.

You'll read more on that in the next chapter. (Don't skip ahead; you might miss something.)

It seems par for the course: I was born without appendages that I could have used. The parts that I do have would turn out crooked or misshaped. And later, I'd grow things that I didn't want.

Most unusual, isn't it?

If it's anything, it's an Amy thing—unscripted, unrehearsed, and patent protected.

My teeth were always crooked since grade school. As mentioned, they've also been susceptible to easy chipping due to excessive use and occasional rough treatment. And during my high school years, I began to develop lesions on my face.

Quite a combo package.

Concerning my birth diagnosis, it was evident that I couldn't do anything about my limbless condition other than to accept it as is and move forward. But I had often desired straight teeth and to be rid of the lesions, which had grown to total three in number. A hat-trick of lumps, I suppose.

By my teen years, however, I had developed a fear of dentists. And I figured the growths were there to stay.

Later, I came to understand that the lesions could be surgically removed. I would sometimes think about that and also consider the idea of having my teeth straightened. But by then, I had matured in my thinking.

First of all, both procedures would be cosmetic, and I assumed my insurance wouldn't cover either of them. Of more significance is that I struggled with the whole idea because I realized that the reason I wanted the procedures was out of vanity. I concluded that I must completely accept and love myself the way God made me—limbless here, lesions there, crooked teeth and all.

I remember feeling a little vain while discussing these things with my friend, Ulf, years ago. He asked if these outward cosmetic upgrades were things that I wanted more than maintaining my faith and upholding a close relationship with God. He also reinforced the notion that it wasn't terrible that I wanted those physical improvements, but if they were taking priority over God in my life, then I was way off track.

In my soul searching, I knew those things were truly not something that I wanted more than to grow in my faith and relationship with God. And they didn't seem possible to have, anyhow. So, I pushed the ideas to the back of my mind as I had done before.

In 2014, the thoughts surfaced again. I brought up the lesions to Jodi in a casual conversation. She encouraged me to at least look into it and said she'd help in any way she could.

Together we researched some possible dermatologists that might take my insurance. I decided to call Premier Plastic Surgery. They had great reviews and were located in Wexford, not too far away. All the while, I was asking God to open the doors if this was something He wanted for me—and close them and make it completely obvious if it wasn't.

What I've always desired most is for His will to be done.

Amazingly, the doors seemed to fly wide open.

Everything just happened so quickly, one event on top of another and thrown into a blender.

Shortly before I scheduled a consultation appointment with Premier, I was talking with Eric about my next speaking engagement, which would be at Pine-Richland Middle School. For some reason, he started telling me these stories about a dentist that he likes and has been friends with for years.

I'm not sure how he managed to spin the conversation in that particular direction other than the fact that he's Eric. (And you know he's been struck by lightning, don't you?)

Furthering the anomalous banter, he then asked if I needed a dentist. Hopefully it wasn't because he had noticed a glob of spinach stuck between my teeth, especially since I don't really eat spinach. But yes, actually; I was somewhat "between dentists" at the time and in need of one.

I divulged to Eric that I'd like to have my teeth straightened but that I was apprehensive about dental work. And that concluded the strange segment of our conversation.

A few days later, Eric came to assist and support me at my Pine-Richland speaking engagement. He had also invited a guest—his friend and dentist, Dr. David Gornick.

Who does that? Who travels around with their dentist? More importantly, why was Dr. Gornick not in Charlotte when I preferred a good tooth extraction over going on stage to do a public speech?

My schedule at Pine-Richland required me to speak twice that day—first to the 7th graders, and then to the 8th graders. Before my first speech, Eric introduced me to Dr. Gornick. He and I chatted and got to know each other a little. We met up and spoke again, for a few minutes, during the break between my presentations.

Unbeknownst to me at the time, he and Eric had been talking about how they might get me into braces, but he couldn't promise Eric anything.

While awaiting my initial consultation with Premier, I went to Dr. Gornick's office for a scheduled cleaning, routine dental exam, and updated x-rays. He was very thorough. I'm sure he removed any leftover spinach that he may have encountered.

Dr. Gornick also discovered a cavity that would have to be filled. So, we made another appointment for that and spent some additional time just talking, and I soon went on my merry way.

All was well until we got a few miles down the road. It was then that I felt a surge of panic. But it wasn't because I knew I'd have to return for a filling; it was because I suddenly realized I didn't settle up with the receptionist for my out-of-pocket cost. I never even asked what I owed for the visit, concerning that which isn't covered by my insurance. It had simply slipped my mind. Apparently, Mom's mind is just as slippery because she never thought of it, either.

To be fair to Eric, I have to wonder of myself:

Who does that? It's one thing to hang out with your dentist and invite him to public speeches, but who absconds with oral exams, x-rays, and spinach removal? Seriously, who shoplifts dental work? Only me, right? Why didn't any alarms go off? Why was there not a buzzer or an electronic warning device of some kind? Where were the ringing bells and flashing lights? How could they have let me escape without blowing a referee's whistle or firing a warning shot? They could have at least thrown a net over me.

From my position, it didn't look good for any of us. With Dad having been waiting behind the wheel of the van as he always does, I'm sure it could have been perceived that he was merely positioned as my getaway driver.

Surely, a state trooper will be stopping us at any moment, with weapon drawn and backup en route. Will Dad be arrested as a co-conspirator? Would Mom be considered an accessory to the crime? Will we be allowed one phone call? If so, can I order a pizza, hold the spinach? Is my offense a misdemeanor charge or a felony? Will my dental insurance cover a defense attorney, or should I just enter an Alford plea?

Feeling completely stupid, inconsiderate, and mortified, I immediately called Dr. Gornick's office to apologize and to ask what I owed. Fortunately, it took little convincing that I wasn't trying to do some sort of grab-and-go of their services or perpetrate any type of intentional wrongdoing.

Among his services, Dr. Gornick had also aligned me with an orthodontist that he recommended, Dr. Thomas Forrest, who would determine if I was a viable candidate for braces. Turned out, I was. My first visit at his office was exceptional. He and his staff couldn't have possibly made me feel more welcome and relaxed than they did.

During that appointment, we discussed the details of me still having a lonely, straggling baby tooth that had never grown up and moved out like its older siblings had done. This lingering upper cuspid was blocking my adult tooth from coming in. The time had come to part with it; the tooth would have to come out.

Shouldn't that have been done in Charlotte?

Also, it would be necessary to have my wisdom teeth removed, all of which were fully impacted. Apparently, eliminating these teeth would make my braces more…bracier, or something. (Sorry, I didn't go to Dentist-lady school any more than Mom went to Nurse-lady school.)

In the juggling of my doctor visits and assorted inquiries, I called Premier and learned that they do take my insurance. Before long, I met with a dermatologist there and was told it was possible to have the lesions removed—and my insurance would cover it! I immediately scheduled the surgery for a week later.

Unlike most things with me, the process fell together quite easily. So much so that Mom decided to see if it was possible for her to have a couple of lumps removed from her scalp as well. We both ended up having outpatient surgery, in succession, on the same day, in the same room. Sort of a two-for-one special.

I asked her, jokingly, "Must we do *everything* together?"

English writer Charles Caleb Colton said, "Imitation is the sincerest form of flattery."

So, I probably should be flattered by it.

The surgeries were performed on September 2nd, just weeks before my bucket list and birthday weekend. Afterwards, Dad took us to lunch at Eat 'N Park for being so good and brave throughout the whole thing.

There I was in a public restaurant with absolutely no makeup on, which is an extremely rare sight in itself. I had stitches all over my face like game lacerations on a hockey goalie, and I was starting to develop a black eye. But I was happy to be rid of the lesions. And I was thankful that everything had gone so well for Mom and me.

During my wait to have the stitches removed, I returned to Dr. Gornick's office for my filling. He worked carefully to avoid contact with my incisions.

A short time later, I went back to Dr. Forrest for what was supposed to be a consultation. To my surprise, however, I was fitted with my upper braces on that very day. I was hoping for Invisalign because they are much less noticeable. They also resemble a hockey mouth guard, which would be appropriate to follow my hat-trick and goalie look.

But Dr. Forrest preferred traditional braces for my situation and chose white ceramic with regular silver wires. Though they were his preference over mine, I was okay with compromising. I was thrilled to have the opportunity to have straight teeth. And the financial part of it all worked out wonderfully, which was an added blessing.

My next step was to have my baby tooth and wisdom teeth extracted as soon as physically possible. No big deal, right?

Well, for a small person, I've been known to generate some big problems at times. For those in the dental world who didn't already know that about me, they were in for a rude awakening, similar to a 3:00 a.m., cold winter rude awakening.

You see, there's no easy way to administer an IV in my scrawny, limbless little self. So, I'd have to undergo a procedure that was more of the traditional hospital outpatient variety.

There it is. That's more like it. Those are the types of complications that I'm used to.

If you'd want to get into a whole "ratio and proportions" thing, it would practically qualify as major surgery for me. Aside from that, I also had speaking engagements to fulfill and lots of artwork to finish.

Concerning the oral surgery, I had little wiggle room in my schedule. I decided to have the work done on Tuesday, a mere two days before Thanksgiving, in spite of the fact that it's a holiday known and loved by all for its identity with intense overeating.

After a lengthy wait, opening ceremonies, and pregame warm-ups, I eventually climbed into the hospital bed and changed into a hideous, unfashionable, no-size-fits-all surgical gown. I then waited some more.

During that time, I also did what any normal girl would do in this day and age; I took a selfie and uploaded it to social media, wearing no makeup!

What's gotten into me?

To be clear about it, Mom actually took the picture, but it fully qualified as a selfie in Amy's world.

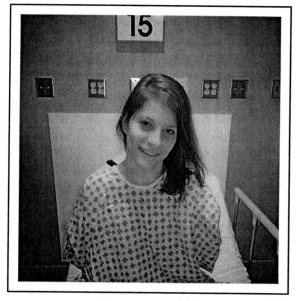

Pre-surgery selfie!

Person after person came into the room asking the same medical questions, over and over. Being the clown that she is, Mom essentially turned it into a circus, announcing that I was an author and handing out my bookmarks to everyone in her reach.

There was one recurring question that repeatedly stumped each of the hospital staff. "Where do they normally check your blood pressure when you go to the doctor?"

"They don't," I said.

But none of them could wrap their minds around that. One by one, they came and went, interrogating me like Eric and John had done. The only thing missing was a .22 rifle.

And a satisfactory answer, of course.

Apparently, all of these staffers had taken creative writing courses and some cross-examination classes because each of them began asking me the same question again, in other ways, using different wordings and various phrases. But my answer was the same.

"They don't check my blood pressure," I said. "They just skip it."

It's as if I don't have any blood pressure. Or, maybe they assume I do and that it's fine. Either way, this was going to be a problem for the surgical team. They would need the ability to monitor my blood pressure while in surgery, so they'd know if I was doing okay. But my body didn't want to cooperate with them.

Mom jokingly suggested placing the blood pressure cuff around my neck. Is it any wonder that she doesn't work in the medical field?

After another long wait, the anesthesiologist came to insert my IV port. For some reason, I was assuming that I'd be asleep during this. I was thinking they would place a gas mask on me and administer a hearty dose of nitrous oxide, some low-grade ethanol, or maybe a blast of diesel fumes, to put me under before inserting such a substantial needle. So, I was surprised when I saw him enter the room with the intention of spearing me.

This is the kind of stuff my fears are made of. Having no long, vein-filled arms to offer, the port would be inserted into my neck. And I'd have to be conscious during it.

I knew I was no longer a two-year-old screaming like a miniature maniac as a medical team held me down to do this once before, but I still had those memories.

The anesthesiologist tilted the bed backwards to where I was practically upside down. He instructed me to take a deep breath and hold it. There was a little pinch from the needle, and then I felt nothing. The port was in, and that was it.

No pain!

Thank you, Sir. Nice doing business with ya.

After being returned to my original upright position and waiting there for a couple of hours, I was finally wheeled into surgery. When the anesthesia was injected into my IV port, I immediately felt my condition change.

"Wow, that stuff works fast!" I blurted.

Oral surgeon Dr. David Dattilo was set to perform my operation. The surgical team quickly began searching for an adequate vein to insert another port, similar to the IV, by which to monitor my blood pressure. One consideration was my armpit region.

Though it wasn't extremely painful, the prodding and poking was quite uncomfortable for me and probably for them also.

I was feeling pretty dopey and more than the usual Snow White version. But knowing they were having trouble finding a good vein, I threw my two cents worth in and began suggesting different areas they could try. I also offered other necessary ramblings and recounted how that, when I was younger, a doctor took a blood draw from a vein in my groin area…

Apparently, the surgical team grew tired of my incoherent chitchatting because next thing I knew I was out cold. Actually, I was just beginning to wake up and realized that I was being wheeled down the hallway, to recovery.

I remember rationalizing that there was no way they could have finished the surgery so quickly. (I didn't know that I had actually gone under; I thought I had been awake the whole time.) Feeling around in my mouth with my tongue, I located the hole in the upper front where my cuspid had been removed. I was surprised that there was no pain and that I felt nothing different in the back where my wisdom teeth were supposed to have been extracted.

Repeatedly comparing the front with the back, I reported my findings to the nurse who was escorting my gurney ride to the recovery room.

"I think they made a mistake," I said. "I think they forgot to take my teeth out!"

The nurse stated, "I wasn't in the room during the surgery. You'll have to ask your parents."

I thought her response was the silliest thing I'd ever heard.

My parents weren't in the room either. How would they know?

Realizing that I was still quite loopy and half asleep, I felt around again to confirm that I wasn't mistaken or going crazy. It didn't feel any different; there was no void in my gums as I thought there should have been.

Sensing another presence beside me, I repeated my concern to whomever it was, announcing that I thought they had made a mistake. Turns out it was the same woman. Again she echoed the same response, "I wasn't in the room during the surgery. You'll have to ask your parents."

Why is she saying this?

I couldn't understand it for the life of me. I'm aware Mom was all dressed up as "Nurse Janet" in my first book. But I'm sure this nurse hadn't even read it. If she had, she'd know Mom isn't a real nurse and wasn't in the operating room. The same is true of Dad.

How would my parents know what happened in there?

Not long after, Mom and Dad came into the recovery room, and I wasted no time launching my investigation. They informed me that the surgical team was unable to find a suitable place to monitor my blood pressure, and I was under anesthesia far too long without being monitored.

The outcome was that Dr. Dattilo had only removed my baby tooth. He *did not* remove my wisdom teeth.

Hah! I might be loopy, but I'm not crazy!

By this time, it was almost five in the evening. We had been there all day. I had been injected, drugged, jabbed, and poked. All of that to only have a little baby tooth pulled!

The discharge nurse told us that we could leave if I was awake enough.

Yep, I'm good.

I got dressed and into my wheelchair. Dad would be my designated driver because he knew I was still under the influence and was probably worried that I'd be slapped with an OVI on the way out.

The man is a retired trucker, an owner/operator who has logged an unfathomable amount of hours at the helm of a monstrous eighteen-wheeler. He safely transported loads of steel all over the country. All he had to do was walk slowly beside my wheelchair and operate the hand controls for me.

As easy as that seems, he kept stopping and starting and jerking and weaving like the drunkard that we had accused him of being. This made my head dizzy, and I had no choice but to relieve him of his duties.

"Can I please drive myself?" I asked.

With Mom biting her nails in anticipation of a lawsuit for me running someone over, I maneuvered my wheelchair flawlessly down the hospital corridors, turned and backed into a crowded elevator, drove to the van, and pulled onto the lift. I then stopped on one of those proverbial dimes that someone may or may not have dropped there.

With that, I was faced with only one problem. It lay directly ahead—literally—in the form of unforgiving metal.

Fearing that I wouldn't have much body strength after surgery, Dad had wrapped my stretchy belt around me, as if he were synching a load of steel, and high enough that it wouldn't allow me to lean forward, at all. This meant I was unable to bend and duck my head as needed, to properly clear the entrance while driving into the van. Before I could vocalize my concern, Dad grabbed the joystick, drove me forward, and rammed my head into the metal doorway.

Yeah, that left a mark.

But the van was okay.

I think I even cried a little. Not so much from the pain, but from the frustration of still being drugged enough that I wasn't able to get out what I wanted to say. And it wasn't especially thrilling that we had all gone through so much—the surgical team, my parents, and me—and the only achievement on the entire day was the removal of a baby tooth that shouldn't have even still been there in the first place.

Before we had left the hospital, the anesthesiologist informed us that, even though I didn't have the full procedure done, I'd still experience a good amount of oral pain. But I didn't. They had written me a script for pain meds, and though I probably could have used them for the concussion Dad gave me, I never took any. And less than forty-eight hours later, I fully enjoyed a complete Thanksgiving dinner.

As is the case every year, I had many reasons to give thanks. I was thankful that I had only a moderate level of soreness and no real pain to speak of. And I was thankful for the retooling that had taken place on my behalf, over the past two months or so.

But I was assuming I'd have to go through the surgical process and blood pressure dilemma again, to have my wisdom teeth extracted.

Shortly after Thanksgiving, I went back to Dr. Forrest, so he could attach a chain between my braces wire and my adult tooth, which would help the tooth come down as it should. On that visit, he announced that I wouldn't have to have my wisdom teeth removed! That was something else to be thankful for.

The final step of this retooling project would be adding my lower braces. The only downside—if you'd want to consider it one—is that my work in paper tole had to be suspended until my time in braces was fulfilled because I couldn't continue to place that kind of pressure on my teeth and gums.

Hence, my "re-tole-ing" would have to wait.

But my artwork would move forward through other methods. Digital formats, for example, require more finesse than force. Because of my circumstances and Alex's generosity in allowing me to borrow his Wacom tablet, my digital drawings and paintings improved, significantly.

In reflection, I could see the hand of God in all the fine details along the way and in allowing everything to come together as it did. And what seemed to be trouble for the doctors in the operating room—forgoing the excavation of my wisdom teeth—was God looking out for me the whole time and sparing me unnecessary suffering.

All of this has reminded me that He is a God of overdoing. Reaching beyond our necessary provisions and daily needs, sometimes He chooses to simply bless us with the things we want. Just because He can.

26

Chin Zits and Spiders

Despite the listed blessings that have come my way and the good fortune that has overtaken me at times, a recent astrological study has positively concluded that the earth doesn't rotate around Amy Brooks. The sun is the physical core of our universe, not me.

I believe God created everything around us and beyond us. I am merely a speck. I don't need much. I try not to ask for things, and I demand nothing special. Therefore, I've never been a sign-carrying advocate of any self-entitlement agenda.

However, as stated in our Declaration of Independence, I do *"hold these truths to be self-evident, that all men are created equal, that they are endowed by their Creator with certain unalienable Rights, that among these are Life, Liberty and the pursuit of Privacy in the bathroom."*

Okay, I fudged that last part a little. Still, it shouldn't be too much to ask. Is it unreasonable for a lady to want some solitude within the borders of her own tinkletorium? That wasn't the case when a particular incident occurred, one autumn afternoon in 2013.

I was in there on that day, minding my own business. Then again, who else's business would I be minding in the bathroom?

Regardless, I thought I was alone, as I should have been. All was well, or so I thought. Suddenly, I saw the movement of a prowling shadow and realized that I was in the presence of some undesirable company. I was being stalked.

I saw him lurking in the corner, startling me at first.

He didn't belong there. Much, like Charles Cornwallis in Charlotte, he was an intruder—completely uninvited and entirely unwelcomed.

The "he" of which I speak was not an archaic British soldier who had come to conquer the city in battle; he was a hideous eight-legged beast, a member of the Arachnids, a revolting creature commonly known as a spider.

Yet, there was nothing common about him.

This evil trespasser was about the size of a Fiat. But he was slightly uglier than a Fiat. Our eyes met when I spotted him, and he displayed an evil Mr. Grinch-like smile.

Many of you know me as a shy, conservative, somewhat apprehensive individual. But not on this day! I wouldn't be intimidated. There would be no backing down.

It's on! We are gonna do this!

An Old West showdown done Pittsburgh style.

At that point, he could only wish to retreat as Cornwallis had done. Apparently, he didn't know any better.

When he sized me up, I heard him snicker. That was just before I squashed him the only way I know how...with my chin.

That's how it's done in these parts, people!

Well, that's how Amy does it. I took it from a page in the user's guide: *Tetraphocomelia For Dummies.*

Don't worry about the hygienics; I held a tissue in my teeth to provide an absorbent barrier between my skin and the squirting spider juices. As unpleasant as that may sound, it really wasn't.

That's my normal, a small segment of my everyday life.

For me, a dress rehearsal means I have to practice getting dressed.

Welcome to my world.

But this really isn't a chapter about my bathroom, a spider, or struggling with my wardrobe; it's a chapter about perspective. On that, it leaves me wondering how things are in your world. Have you ever schmushed a spider with your chin? I do realize "schmushed" wasn't a proper English word before the writing of this book, but have you ever done that? You might want to try it sometime.

Or maybe not.

If you haven't, it's probably because you've never *had* to exterminate something in that fashion. For me it's commonplace.

I'm wondering about your spider removal method. Do you whack them with a shoe? Do you scoop them up and toss them outside? Unless you are up for an adventure, I would assume your technique involves the use of hands in some way and never your chin. Am I right?

So, how bad do you have it? Do you possess hands with which to eliminate a spider? Do you have feet to facilitate its disposal?

How about this? What do you do at that moment when your contact lenses gain a death grip on your eyeballs? Without using your hands, try to take them out (the contacts, not the eyeballs).

I'm gonna go Vegas odds here and bet you are capable of doing your own hair.

Me? I can sweep out the snarls by trapping a hairbrush in an upper drawer. I then repeatedly glide my head beneath the brush, allowing my hair to flow through the bristles. Other than that, I'm like an equal opportunity employer when it comes to hairstyling. Mom has to shampoo and blow-dry it for me. Dad does the straightening.

What can I say? He's a man of many talents. Trucker, craftsman, hairstylist. Apparently, to him, a straightening iron is just another power tool. He happens to be rather proficient with tools of any kind. Mom is too much of a girl when it comes to that sort of thing. I just can't trust her to straighten my hair properly. And after my early experience with the hot glue gun, neither she nor Dad trusts me to attempt it myself.

I think the reason that their tag team efforts are so effective is because of their personality differences. Mom won't listen to how I want my hair done. She just does it her way. As you learned in my first book, listening is what Dad does best.

He is great at following verbal instructions and hangs in there until it's done the way I like it. You might want to keep him in mind if you ever need someone to straighten your hair. Just don't ask him to do a ponytail because he can't get one right for anything. Mom's the one to call on for those.

You might want to make a note of these things. Like Dad and my hair, you'll have to keep it straight. Well, I have to, anyhow. It's all just part of my daily routine. Tetraphocomelia, remember?

And don't even get me started about how to maintain a proper eating etiquette. That in itself can be a balancing act—the act of using the endpoint of my arm to balance a spoon or fork on the rim of my dish so I can consume its contents.

Whether clearly spoken or simply implied, the message I take to the general public is one of perspective on things like this. Is life really as horrible as you sometimes think it is?

Are you in need of a friendly reminder that your existence contains much more potential than you believe it does, in spite of whatever challenges you may face?

There are things that we have to get used to, and there are things that we just have to get over. I wish to help with those things, desiring to inject a shot of hope where needed (without the painful itch at the injection site).

Sure, we all get the mulligrubbs at times, but we don't have to let them get us. We can overcome our circumstances. We can conquer adversity. We can "get over it."

Everyone is subjected to the law of gravity, but we can also counter it with the law of lift. I hope to offer some of that lift.

Actually, God does the heavy work; ultimately, it is He Who does the lifting—with His unseen arms.

Let's narrow the lens on this a bit. To you teens, I ask a bonus question: What's on your chin? A dead spider? Probably not. Some acne perhaps? Likely. What's the big deal? Is a chin zit really the end of the world?

Someone might say your ears are too big. Maybe you think your breasts are too small, your nose is crooked, or you are wrapped in the wrong skin tone.

Too tall, too thin, too short, too heavy. Bad teeth, bad nails, fat body, fat chance. Too much this, not enough that. Lacking here, failing there. Not smart enough, not good enough, not strong enough, not pretty enough. Whatever. But I get it. I understand. Sometimes I struggle with thoughts or feelings such as these, too. I also have made it my choice, my daily decision, to fight them off and give them no room in my life.

Those things are rubbish. It's all just empty sound, meaningless chatter, annoying static. It's white noise from a blackened mindset. A distraction from reality, a diversion from the truth. They are all lies because none of it really matters. It doesn't accurately define who you are or project the value of your true worth.

As the sun is the core of our universe, that's basically the core of my message.

In a society of collective hopelessness, I mean to inspire you to rise up and succeed. In a world of widespread apathy, I urge you to be accountable.

I challenge you to accept responsibility. I invite you to receive healing. I call you to come forward and move onward.

The decision to share my run-in with the spider was not for the sake of simply telling a story; it was for the sake of asking an imperative question:

Which would you rather have on your chin, a passing zit that you can easily treat with ointment or a flattened dead spider because you have no hands to deal with it otherwise?

Basically, it comes down to the basics.

It's the small things—both positive and negative—that often end up being big. Restricted self-awareness, shattered confidence, and feelings of inferiority are things that can cripple us if ignored or allowed to persist.

Are you letting something as insignificant as a zit to distort your self-worth? Do you give credence to those who say you are destined to fail or that you cannot accomplish your goals, fulfill your purpose, or live out your dreams?

That's what was said of me when I was born. And that's why my birth parents walked out and left me at the hospital.

Do I forgive them for that?

Well…no, actually.

I feel there is really nothing to forgive.

There is no offense to either retain or release.

I hold no bitterness towards my birth parents or my birth family, whatsoever. For one thing, I was a newborn; I remember nothing of what happened. I was never emotionally scarred or harmed in any way by their decision. And I was too young to feel any hurt over it.

Furthermore, I wasn't tossed into a dumpster or haphazardly placed on the front porch of a rundown mobile home; I was left in a hospital—a safe, sanitary environment where I was fed, bathed, and clothed.

My abandonment was just a small part of a much larger picture and better situation. It was a catalyst toward a greater and permanent acceptance. It was a momentary shard of God's overall plan for my life. The Brooks family *chose* me!

As for the professionals, the doctors, the experts—yes, some agreed that I'd never amount to anything, that I'd never learn to do anything for myself, that I'd never have anything to offer—I have no animosity about any of that. Because these were predictions based on a very unique, unfamiliar, and difficult case.

By the grace of God and through His strength, my negative prognosis was proven wrong. Yours can be also. Like acne, circumstances such as these are treatable blemishes of life.

They are zits—annoying but curable.

Or, you can think of them as nothing more than irritating spiders, just waiting to be schmushed.

27

Curtain Rod Hydration

Between three classes of people—the thirsty, the sleepy, and the criminally foolish who live next door—I have made a noteworthy discovery that might be good to pass along: if you seek potable hydration in Pittsburgh, the use of divination is completely unnecessary. Dowsing rods are simply not needed here. This finding came to me, unexpectedly, on a Friday afternoon in April 2015.

That day began with me fulfilling a speaking engagement in Sewickley, at The Watson Institute. Formerly known as D.T. Watson, this is the same place that helped me with prosthetic ideas and physical therapy sessions when I was an infant.

When we returned home from the institute, Mom made mini pizzas for lunch. She then sprawled out to take a nap on the living room sofa. Dad headed upstairs to do the same.

That's what people do after they've raised their kids and retired from work and eaten too many mini pizzas; they nap. And my parents are good at it.

Myself, I had other things to do. So, I went up to my room to do whatever it was that was so pressing at the time.

If you look at a family portrait of all the Brooks people, you can easily tell who it is among us that need their beauty sleep. Okay, I can use a little, but compared to…

Well, we'll just leave it at that.

What's important is that I didn't need a nap. But sleep is merely a secondary byproduct of this chapter; water is the main ingredient, and silliness is my central thesis.

That day, April 10, was National Sibling's Day on social media, so Myia and I started texting with each other about that. With she and her family living directly next door to us, our text messages didn't have far to travel. And we sent them in quick succession. Little did I know how greatly beneficial our living location would become in just a short time.

As I puttered around my room and carried on our texting dialog, I began to realize how thirsty I was. In fact, I soon felt completely parched.

Probably from all the hot air that I had spouted at Watson.

Forget about that whole "April showers" thing. It was a beautiful day with not a cloud in the sky. Besides, a spring shower would do nothing inside our dry house. And having no hands would do nothing in my desire to quench my relentless thirst.

With Dad napping upstairs and Mom presumably asleep downstairs, the connecting point between my parents was my chairlift, which bore the potential of waking them.

Though not nearly as loud as *Daddy's Nightmare*, when the house is quiet and someone is sleeping, my chairlift does contain the audible equivalent of a slow-moving passenger train—designed for only one passenger, of course.

So, the noise was an immediate concern of mine.

The only faucets I can reach are in my bathroom, which is downstairs. And we only drink bottled or filtered water, anyhow. So, the dilemma was that of how I might obtain a bottle of cool, refreshing H_2O.

Having mentioned to Myia how incredibly thirsty I was, I jokingly asked if she could throw me a glass of water through the window. I should have known better than to suggest something like that to Myia, as her brain immediately went into creative/fix-it/challenge mode.

One might expect that she could have simply walked a bottle of water over to our house, but it really wasn't a viable option. Though I didn't hear anything reverberating off the living room walls or feel any vibrations through the floorboards, I assumed, by this time, Mom was in a deep sleep, in a dense forest, sawing fresh redwoods trees. If Myia would enter the house, it would surely awaken our Sleeping Beauty, and neither of us wanted to risk it.

With my bathroom window being in closest alignment with the windows on our side of her house, Myia began considering the idea of tossing a bottled water to me.

"Can you open your bathroom window?" she asked.

I replied that I could open it by climbing onto my toilet, but the screen would be a challenge. And Myia's bottle throwing skills were largely unproven. Even she admitted that her aim might be off and she'd shatter the window, instead of hitting the open space beneath it. Knowing Myia, that would be a very real possibility.

Besides, going downstairs on my passenger train would likely awaken Mom and Dad, which would defeat the entire purpose. Our objective was to satisfy my thirst without stirring our parents.

So, that brought the strike count to three with the bottle throwing idea. We'd surely have to come up with something else. Myia took this as a personal challenge that she was bound to accomplish.

It's quite possible that I've picked up some of my determination and competitiveness from her. We were in it together, Myia and me. There was no in between; we'd either strike water or I'd wilt and wither from dehydration.

With the bottom window ruled out, our thoughts shifted to my bedroom. I told her I could open the window, but, like my bathroom, the screen was still a dilemma. And as I was fading from thirst, Myia's throwing confidence was fading even faster.

I seriously was *super* thirsty and was thinking there'd be no way she could get water over to me. I then got a text from Myia who had moved to her upstairs window. Her message read, "Look out your window. Can you see me?"

Climbing onto my bed, which is under the window facing Myia and Mike's house, I pulled back the curtains. But I couldn't lift the blinds because the pull string is near the top.

In the meantime, I tucked myself behind the blinds.

Having my cell phone with me, I called Myia's number.

So, there I was, at my bedroom window, with Venetian blinds draped down my back, on my phone, talking to Myia as we looked over at one another.

We couldn't help but to giggle like a couple of teenagers. How could we not find humor in such a predicament, especially while "Skyping" through neighboring windows?

If that particular scenario isn't ridiculous enough for you, stay with me; it gets better.

Myia instructed me, via cell phone, to open the window. Not knowing if the casing was locked or unlocked, I placed my phone on the sill and pushed upward with my arm. The windowpane moved just far enough for me to wedge my head beneath it. Using the power of positive thinking (my skull), I then opened the window as far as I could.

With that accomplishment, we hung up our phones and could freely talk through our open windows. But time was running out. I could sense the buzzards circling the rooftop as Myia and I discussed possible methods for getting me water.

The next point of business was to determine if I could open the screen. My recollection was that it was locked at the top. I didn't expect the thing to budge, but to my surprise it did. Just a little. The screen seemed free enough to open, but I couldn't reach any further to push it up more than a couple of inches.

Myia asked if I had a stick or something to use for an extension. For a minute, I couldn't think of anything that would be long enough. And then, I remembered having a dressing stick that I use solely for straightening Logic's bed at night.

I climbed out from behind the blinds, scooted off the bed, grabbed the dressing stick, propped it on the bed, climbed back up, snaked my way behind the blinds, and used the stick to open the screen. It was another achievement, but the added exercise increased my thirst all the more.

Surely, the buzzards had landed by then.

We both agreed that throwing the water bottle through the window was not a feasible option. If her aim was bad, she'd break the window. If her aim was good, she'd damage the blinds. Either way, we'd have to explain to Dad how two adult women managed to cause such damage by trying to get a drink of water.

"If I can find a tube long enough, I could slide the water through the tube and into your window," says Myia. "Hold on, I'll be back."

So, I waited for what seemed like forever, expecting to keel over from dehydration. Myia finally returned to the window. No tube. But she tells me she has a curtain rod.

A curtain rod?

Why not a dowsing rod?

She left Myia Kohnen and came back Martha Stewart.

A curtain rod.

Excuse me, Miss Martha, are we gonna drink water or decorate windows?

But Martha/Myia assured me that she had a plan: she would place a bottled water inside a hand basket, hang the basket from the curtain rod, and extend it to my window.

It didn't seem like the brightest of ideas, but it was all we had to work with at the moment, and I really, really needed that water.

First, we decided to gage the length the curtain rod. So, here it comes, a thin metal extendable shaft, from her window to mine.

I also saw a wad of white duct tape in the middle.

Not one, but two curtain rods taped together.

But even at double the length, the invention came up a little short.

Back to the drawing board.

If only we had that tube.

I then realized I still had the dressing stick tucked under my arm and thought I might be able to use it to fill in the gap between the curtain rod and my window. If Myia could get the basket close enough, I was confident I could hook it with the stick and haul it inside.

"Yea, that's a great idea. Let's try it!"

So, Myia pulled the curtain rod back to her side and hooked the basket onto the end of it. She then placed the bottle into the basket and started feeding it over to me.

Here it came, pretty as a picture!

About halfway between the two houses, I started to get excited and could almost taste the cool, soothing liquid gliding down my dusty throat.

Myia's plan was working!

And then, it wasn't.

All of a sudden, the curtain rod began to bend at the joint, lowering the basket and my water toward the earth. The only thing that could have made it funnier is if we would have had a cartoonish "drooping" sound effect as the rod bent completely in half.

What a letdown, literally.

The weight was obviously too much for the flimsy rod and duct tape joint, and it was all Myia could do to drag the basket back up and into her window.

That's how I remember it, anyhow. At that point, severe dehydration had taken hold. It could have all been a mirage. Maybe I wasn't in my room in Pittsburgh; maybe I was crawling helplessly through the Mojave Desert, entertaining a silly hallucination of my sister trying to serve me a bottle of water from a bent curtain rod and faltering duct tape.

The distant slurping sound I began to hear were the buzzards licking their lips. (For those of you who have never thirsted to the point of hallucination, it's equivalent to a dream or a cartoon in that anything can happen and everything is possible. It just so happens that, in my mirage, buzzards do have lips, okay?)

The sound of Myia's voice brought me out of my weltering trance. Again it was the tube idea. Though it seemed like the perfect solution, the perfect tool for the job, we didn't have one.

Perhaps it was the tube that was a mirage.

Once and for all, we had to erase it from our minds and think of something else. As we discussed other ideas, Myia ducked down and disappeared from the window again.

Great, am I gonna get Martha Stewart or Bob the Builder?

You just never know with Myia.

It only took a few minutes for me to correctly guess Bob the Builder. The hint came when I heard biff! bang! boom! followed by a loud "Ouch!" from Myia.

And then there was silence.

What's going on?

I can't see anything!

Myia was nowhere in sight, but next thing I know, here comes the curtain rod poking out of her window again…with an excessive amount of duct tape wrapped at the joints…and a third curtain rod attached!

No more messing around, right?

Count 'em! Three curtain rods!

And probably as many rolls of duct tape holding them together!

That was certainly long enough reach.

For added stability, I offered the idea of me holding onto my end of the rod while she held onto the other. And then, we might let the basket slide across the rods, like it's on a trolley.

After exhausting all other possibilities, this seemed like a workable plan. But it did come with some concerns. I was afraid that the basket wouldn't slide over the gaudy mounds of tape, or that the tape just wouldn't hold and everything would go crashing to the ground.

Myia poked the long, flimsy rod over to my window, and I secured my end of it the best I could by trapping it between my left shoulder and my chin. To be ready to make the grab, I held the dressing stick under my right arm.

Before trying to send the basket over, Myia first wanted me to feel the weight of the contents so I could get an idea of how heavy it would be and guess how hard I'd have to hold onto the rod as the cargo approached.

From inside the window, she slid the basket handle onto her end of the rod and allowed the basket to hang there with the water in it. When I was ready, she let go of the basket and lifted her end of the curtain rod.

Suddenly and surprisingly, the basket came flying over to me, all the way to the window!

I couldn't believe it.

Now all I had to do was continue holding the rod on my left shoulder and hook the dressing stick onto the basket with my right arm.

Easier said than done, but I was able to manage it.

Using the tiny knobs on the dressing stick to hook it, I grabbed the basket handle and pulled it toward me. But when I tried to lift the basket over the outer windowsill, the stick lost its hold. This happened repeatedly. I would hook the basket, try to haul it over the ledge, and the stick would come unhooked, time after time.

I was so close to having water…

Finally, I realized that I didn't have to get the whole basket in the window; if I continued what I was doing and used the window to my advantage, I could tilt the basket and let the bottle roll onto the sill where I could haul it in with my arm. After a couple of tries, it worked!

Just as I had struck water, my nephew, Cameron, came home and couldn't help but laugh at the strange predicament that his mom and Aunt Amy were in.

Being proud of our achievement, we asked him to take a picture. It made a good National Siblings Day post on social media.

Though Cameron thought it was all quite funny, you don't have to worry about what any neighbors or passing pedestrians might have thought. Considering the houses involved and the people who live in them, I'm sure they never batted an eye.

With the picture taken and my coveted bottle of water tucked beneath my chin, I climbed off the bed with the task of having to remove the cap.

Normally, I'm good at it. I just bite down and rotate my lower jaw in a counterclockwise motion. This has worked well for items such as bottled water and toothpaste. I have even been able to open medicine bottles said

Martha Stewart delivers

to be "child proof" on labeling that should not read as such if they aren't "Amy proof."

But wearing braces made that particular task much more difficult. So, Mom or Dad would usually break the seal for me.

After the long, drawn-out ordeal Myia and I had gone through, I wasn't about to let weak, sensitive teeth and a tight bottle cap deprive me of hydration. It took only a few times—biting down and twisting—and I got it!

With the bottleneck clenched in my teeth, I threw my head back and set a world's record for drinking a pint of water. And the buzzards had no choice but to fly off to someone else's rooftop.

Later, I went downstairs because, of course, I had to pee after chugging my water.

How smart am I, right?

After calculating my decreased level of intelligence, you'll have to deduct a few more points when you learn of my conversation with Mom. Having heard the upstairs commotion, she asked, "What were you *doing* up there?"

I proceeded to tell her the story about my water bottle adventure and how I didn't want to awaken her or Dad over it.

As noble as that was, Mom informed me that she had never fallen asleep. She was awake the entire time, listening. She had heard all the chatter and giggling, all the rustling and moving about. Every, bump, thump, and scrape.

All the while, Mom assumed Logic and I were just roughhousing, but she never went to investigate. Then again, why would she? She had done that once when I was a baby and found that I was being used for a football. Maybe she had learned her lesson back then and figured some things are better left unknown.

As for my own lesson, what I learned on that April afternoon, 2015, was that you don't need dowsing rods to locate water in Pittsburgh. There's no need to resort to divination or hocus-pocus of any type. A few metal curtain rods will work perfectly in my neighborhood.

28

Personal Effects

S ituations and interactions. It seems these are the primary elements of a life in motion. In other words: things that happen and individuals we encounter. Certainly, the details will differ for each of us, but the translation is the same.

For me, it can be trying to secure a simple bottle of drinking water while battling amusing but ridiculous circumstances. At other times, it's a stalking, creepy spider. Or, it could be the woman in the parking lot of the U.S. Post Office, such as the one I observed on a cold day in February 2014.

It was a time when all eyes should have been focused half a world away as the winter Olympics were ramping up in Russia. Everyone was watching them.

Or so I thought.

One woman was an exception.

Clearly, she was watching me, instead.

Staring actually, like the spider in my bathroom.

But before you even think it, the answer is no; I had no intention of schmushing the woman with my chin, or by any other means. The thought just never entered my mind.

This visual meeting took place while Mom was inside the post office. As Dad and I waited in the van, I sat texting—on that day it was probably with Myia or maybe with my friend, Matt. During our exchanges of words and emoticons and our lexis of OMGs and LOLs and other necessary expressions, I happened to glance over and notice the woman sitting in the car next to us.

And she was completely gawking her eyeballs out.

The look on her face said it all. And it was priceless.

To her, the Olympic Games were nonexistent. She just sat there looking at me, studying my every move. Of course, I didn't have too many moves, but the ones I did use fascinated her, apparently.

The woman seemed quite amazed by my texting method—pointing my upper lip and using it to peck on my phone as I balanced it on my shoulder.

Her eyes were fully dilated, and her mouth hung open like a yawning polar bear. There may have even been a slight trickle of drool slithering from the corner of her mouth, but don't quote me on that.

Drool or not, I couldn't help but to wonder what she was thinking. Later, a friend suggested that I should have spun my head around 360 degrees like an owl, just to mess with her a bit.

After all, luxury jeweler and author Harry Winston once said, "People will stare. Make it worth their while."

However, the result probably wouldn't have been favorable to the woman's sanity. It likely would have freaked her out more than she already was.

Besides, I don't fully have that maneuver perfected yet.

So, I just shrugged and carried on as usual, in my own unusual way.

But what do you suppose was going through her mind? Was she completely baffled? Did she think she was merely seeing things? What affect did it have on her that day?

Your guess is as good as mine.

Maybe even better.

Or, consider little Miss Sadie. She is Eric and Miss Heidi's daughter and was only eight when we first met. Eric brought her over to talk to me one day. Here they came, daddy and daughter, walking hand in hand.

How cute.

Everything was fine until they drew near, and I said hello to her. Seeing me up close—no arms, no legs, a talking human torso—Miss Sadie went limp like a rag doll and just fainted on the spot.

To her, I was probably like some sort of magic trick or the resemblance of a real-life Halloween display. You'll have to trust me on this: I hadn't let out with a rumbling, ghoulish, guttural laugh; she just fainted on her own.

That isn't necessarily the kind of impression I wish to leave with people, particularly small children.

Fortunately, dramatic effects can be overcome.

Miss Sadie has since stopped fainting in my presence.

Among the primary elements of life—things that happen and individuals we encounter—our focus can easily be set upon how things and people affect us from day to day without any more thought than that.

But let's step outside ourselves for a moment.

Let's turn the coin over.

What kind of effect are we having on others?

Granted, things didn't turn out so well for the spider I met. Then again, it was only a hideous member of the arachnid species.

Like that spider or the woman at the post office, we don't always know who is watching us or when they are doing so. And we often are not aware of the effect that we have on those of the human variety.

I've always believed that I was born the way I was for a reason, and it wasn't just all about me. No one had to tell me that or explain it or try to convince me in some way; it was just something that I've known by instinct, from as far back as I can remember. It just came naturally for me to understand that. And it has also been within me, at the core of who I am, to love God and to love people.

What didn't come so easily was the acceptance of things that were often said about me throughout most of my life. When I was little and people would meet me, without fail, they would say I was an inspiration.

I always thought that was silliness, wondering, *How am I an inspiration, especially being so young?*

I hadn't done anything to inspire people. I was just living my life to the best of my ability. And though I fail miserably at times, my desire has been to honor God with my actions and to shine His light in some way.

Though I didn't always know how to do that, Mom would say it was through my daily living, my daily activities that everyone uses their hands and feet for. She explained that because I didn't have those appendages and was achieving my goals, that was what inspired people. And she said my spirit and disposition always shined and showed them Jesus, which was inspiring also.

But I really didn't get it, especially the latter part. Though I consider myself a perfectionist, I am the most imperfect person you'll ever meet. Putting aside the physical imperfections, I am completely capable of faltering when it comes to honoring God as I should. How could Someone like Him shine through someone like me?

As I grew older, I kept hearing the same thing from others; they said I inspired them. But it never made sense to me. It just didn't compute.

There were also many who said I'd write a book someday.

What did they know?

Others predicted that I'd speak to live audiences, sharing my story with them.

More silliness.

Honestly, neither of those things was on my personal radar or bucket list. Writing a book and public speaking are two activities that I had never been interested in.

But sometimes, it takes God Himself to convince us.

When I graduated from high school as a "Jenius," because of being "S-M-R-T," my graduation gift from my parents was twofold—a trip to Disney World and a new *Bible*.

Admittedly, I hadn't done a lot of *Bible* reading before then, because I was just not much of a reader.

It was during that time—away from the distractions and demanding workload of school, in the presence of God and in the quietness of His word—that I began feeling the breath of the Holy Spirit in a fresher, clearer way.

He seemed to impress upon me the notion that maybe the things my mom had been saying about me were true, that the way I lived my life—my attitude toward situations and how I treated people—showed them Jesus.

During those times of deep reflection and wanting to truly understand what my purpose was, I also began to realize how much I loved being an encouragement to people, just someone that friends could come to and vent or unload their worries. Or someone they could rely on when they needed prayer.

I started to think that was my purpose or my calling. I was okay with that, mainly because I was comfortable with it. Any idea of public speaking terrified me, and I never really thought I'd have to do that. For one thing, I wasn't trained or somehow qualified for it.

But a friend of mine often uses this popular phrase: "God doesn't call the qualified; He qualifies the called."

If God calls you to do something, He'll first make it known to you that that's what you're supposed to do. And then, He'll equip you and qualify you to do it.

As a Broadway musical suggests: Your arms are too short to box with God.

I suppose that goes double for me.

So, once I began to understand what He was asking me to do, I had no choice but to surrender to it. After all, what I've always wanted was to do His will and to help others.

But I wanted to somehow do it anonymously and invisibly, not with my name and picture on a book or by being on a stage or at the front of a room with a live audience present. As it is, I've never felt confident in most social situations and certainly never liked receiving attention. I prefer being in the background, unseen an unheard.

But God had other ideas about that.

Though I've now delivered more public speeches than I can count on your fingers and toes, I still get as nervous as the first time. However, there is comfort that follows the nervousness because I know, when it's over, it was God Who got me through it. And each time there has been an overwhelming response. Every presentation has brought tremendous feedback.

And not the microphone kind.

Still, I struggle in knowing that I'm unworthy to have a platform from which to reach out and tell my story.

For each of us, it comes down to finding our calling and being obedient to it, using the tools God has given us to benefit someone else. And there's no expiration date on it; you are never too young or too old to make it happen.

I love to see God working in the lives of others by choosing to bless the tiny morsels that I've offered and allowing it to have a positive effect on people. Of greater significance is that God has made my story His story, which is what I truly want, that He might be glorified in it.

Through it all, I'm learning to just be thankful for His grace, reminding myself that He has forgiven the mistakes of my past, He already knows the ones of my future, and He loves me in spite of those things. This little perfectionist will never be perfect without Him. And I am becoming okay with that because He knows my heart, ultimately and intimately.

And that's what I want to share with others—my heart and the reality of my humanness. I enjoy one-on-one interaction, but sometimes it seems people view me as being without fault when the opposite is actually true.

Among other things, I freak people out in parking lots and cause little kids to lose consciousness. But I'm working on those things.

In the process, I can only strive for something better, something positive, something helpful and constructive, something that has far-reaching value and offers unfailing substance.

Though my memoirs are written in a way that is intended to be engaging and humorous, I hope to offer more than fleeting entertainment. And I'd like my book to point you to a better "book," the one that I received as a graduation gift.

Concerning the woman in the car at the post office, I'll never know what she was thinking or what affect my texting had on her. Hopefully it was something positive.

As for the rest of you, if I make you laugh, I have served a dose of medicine. If I have inspired you, I have honored God. If I offer lasting encouragement, I have made a contribution to life. If I pluck someone from the incinerating flames of despair by nudging them toward the light of Christ and help their faith in Him to be strengthened, I have handed them a portion of something boundlessly greater than myself. These are the things that I can personally offer. This I see as my calling in life.

A line in one of Brett's earlier songs says this:

"If you'd like to shoot the breeze, well, I'm here to listen."

Casual but inviting. It can also be very effective.

If I were a songwriter, I would have written the same thing.

It just so happens Brett beat me to it.

And I'm not a songwriter.

The line accurately describes how I've always felt toward people and renders something that I can offer. The only thing I ask in return is that you don't sit there with your eyeballs popping out and no one faints in my company.

29

Oppositions and Attitudes

The quotation goes like this: "My happiness grows in direct proportion to my acceptance and in inverse proportion to my expectations."

He doesn't claim to be its originator, but that is a line made popular by actor Michael J. Fox. He adopted the saying in his battle with Parkinson's disease, which he began at age thirty.

Though it is an unusually young age for the onset of such a diagnosis, it has been his battle, regardless. And he has maintained a remarkable attitude in the face of that miserable ailment.

From where do these types of mannerisms derive? How are these viewpoints developed? What causes them to grow and produce a healthy lifestyle?

What about our overall personality or general belief system?

Our basic decision-making process?

Our family structure?

Our core values?

Is it safe to assume that these are genetic traits? Would it be accurate to say that, whether good or bad, they are learned behaviors or practices that we've adopted by exposure?

Are we by-products of example?

Forget my lack of limbs for a moment. Do you believe I may have had an advantage in life? I feel that, in many ways, I have.

Sure, things got off to a rough start for me. But to be realistic about it, as a baby I wasn't cognizant to the fact that I was born without limbs. I wasn't aware of my birth parents walking out and leaving me.

It could at least be considered a unique beginning.

As bad as it all may sound, things got better from there. I was brought into a great home and cared for by wonderful people.

Many have been less fortunate in that regard because not every parent out there is a Richard or Janet Brooks. Not every brother or sister is a Brian, Candy, Myia, or Noah. Not every home is of strong morals and sound character.

By this, I've had a great advantage.

But how exactly?

In what precise way?

From my perspective, the answer is quite simple: any good in me is because of God in me. That is the greatest advantage of all. I am truly grateful to have been given that, and I fully realize many have not been as privileged in these things.

I have known kindness. I have experienced goodness.

But are there any guarantees either way?

Are good outcomes exclusive to good influence?

Comparatively, does hardship or undesirable situations mandate a negative result?

Consider my parents. They are good, honest, caring people. They both came from that type of environment; their families possessed those traits and passed them along. You might think of them as lucky or blessed. They could be counted among those who were shined upon by the light of life.

It's a no-brainer, wouldn't you say?

It seems simple; even predictable, perhaps.

People often claim to be products of their environment, something generally referenced in a negative way. They might feel that they are justified in carrying out harmful acts or destructive behaviors because of damaging influence, abuse, or neglect.

Some may believe that wholesome decisions or constructive behaviors are strictly reserved for those who may have had a trouble-free existence or that these traits are the private property of the fortunate few who life has favored. Would you agree?

Let's reflect upon Eric's mom and dad.

Like me, Eric was blessed with incredible parents—a loving and caring couple, people who have continually maintained an impeccable work ethic and great morals.

As teens, they were stable and mature beyond their years. They chose to marry fresh out of high school, and both become very successful in their careers. More importantly, they established a solid marriage and created a warm and tender home.

As parents, they provided what Eric describes as nothing less than a fantasy childhood for him and his sisters. They were always a close-knit family who lacked nothing.

It seems logical to conclude that Eric's mom and dad simply passed down extravagance and qualities inherited from their own parents. Naturally, we might assume that they came from the very type of home environment and core values that they practiced. They must have had an advantage over many others, right?

They did not.

Instead, they created something that they had never had.

Eric's parents married so young for two reasons: not only were they in love, but they also needed to escape.

You see, both had come from horribly abusive homes. Yet, they refused to transfer their childhood hurts into adulthood. They did not repeat the destructive actions that they had seen and known.

Together, they made a deliberate and conscious decision to not allow past bloodline practices to become their own family tradition. They chose to do something different, something better than what they had been subjected to when they were growing up.

As Michael J. Fox has accepted his physical ailment and found happiness in spite of it, Eric's parents accepted their past for what it was, and they moved beyond it in a positive direction.

In different ways and to varying degrees, everyone will face oppositions in life. At some point, the deck will be stacked against you. The odds will not be in your favor. Disadvantage will arrive without warning to sabotage your plans.

Disappointment will come to crush your hopes. Uninvited evil will show up to steal your dreams, impede your progress, or to knock you down, completely.

It could be for only a short duration. You might experience it in fragmented periods of time. Or, it could be the story of your entire life.

Sometimes problems come and go.

Sometimes problems come and stay.

Infesting like a ravenous swarm of termites, trouble seeks to devour our homes and the foundation of our very existence.

What do we do about these things? How do we respond?

Is our happiness based on pleasant occurrences?

Can we find joy and contentment to exist in inverse proportion to our hardships?

Is our attitude defined by our circumstances?

Is our disposition reflected by our experiences?

I believe it all comes down to personal decision-making.

Of truth, it's more a matter of choices than of chances.

Sure, there are many who have suffered horrible experiences and have been put at great disadvantages. These problems were found in the majority of the foster children who came into our home. Today, malice and cruelty persist throughout all of civilization, and I don't intend to minimize that sad reality.

Adversity discriminates against no one. It has appeared to every social status and to all generations. Storms of life have blown in from every direction and have thrust themselves upon all of mankind.

Misfortune has ambushed.

Tragedy has attacked.

Calamity has stricken.

Fear has taken captive.

For many, opposition has been their one companion. Some have known only the worst of what our world has to offer.

Others have been abandoned by parents, forsaken by friends, discarded by society. Spiritually, emotionally, and physically, untold numbers are bruised. Numerous have been battered. Many have been beaten. Scores lie defeated and ignored.

Through it all, choices have to be made.

They may not come in the form of those large-scale, fork-in-the-road types of decisions. Primarily it's the small, everyday, step-by-step things that matter most.

Our paths are often carved by how we handle those momentary things that appear to us. If we are able to face them and respond properly, we are likely to positively react to life's bigger problems.

Michael J. Fox has elected to carry a happiness that runs counter to his affliction. He didn't subscribe to a victim mentality. The same is true of Eric's parents. They chose something greater.

I have, too. This is a choice that I have to make each and every day because it isn't something that comes naturally. It comes down to taking ownership, being responsible for our actions and decisions. As good quotes go, here's a great one from an unknown source—from an anonymous donor, if you will.

Our lives are not determined by what happens to us but by how we react to what happens, not by what life brings to us, but by the attitude we bring to life. A positive attitude causes a chain reaction of positive thoughts, events, and outcomes. It is a catalyst, a spark that creates extraordinary results.

Unfortunately, many individuals, numerous marriages, and countless families are blemished by hurtful situations and damaging circumstances. They are veiled in a smear of transcending greyness.

Lost beneath the shadows of haunting memories.

Scattered by chaos and turmoil.

These might be things to which you can relate. Yet, as cliché as it may sound, someone has it worse than you.

Worse than me, also.

No matter how bad a day we are having, someone near us is experiencing one that is far worse and longer lasting. In spite of your most unfavorable condition, there is someone who would gladly trade places with you.

As for the greyness—that dismal, murky smudge of gloom that reaches onto all—I have had a personal encounter with it. Some of you may not think so. Many of you would not have known. But I have shivered beneath its shadow. I have felt its touch. I have been held in its grip.

I have experienced its merciless sting.

I have tasted its unsavoriness.

And it has tasted me.

I have carried the weight of its yoke, the burden of its darkness. While I am eternally grateful for the light that has pulled me from it, my encounter is something that I have decided to include before bringing my story to a close.

My hope is that it might benefit you or someone you love.

30

Invisible God

There's no need to select a jury. There's no cause for deliberation. We don't have to put it to a vote or leave it to the decision of popular opinion. The evidence is timeless. The proof is indisputable: God, our Master and King, is real. The Lord of heaven and Creator of the earth is alive and well.

He has chosen to love us in spite of ourselves. And He has elected to be involved in even the smallest matters of our lives.

Of the many things that we can learn about God from the *Bible*, we know that He is a spirit. But He also has a literal form, the face of which no mortal man has been permitted to behold. To the naked eye, to the physical realm, and to a darkened world, He remains unseen.

By faith, we see Him in our hearts. By experience, we find Him in our lives. By encounter and by interaction, we know Him. We believe God for what He says. We trust Him for what He does. We worship Him for Who He is.

Though it makes no sense to me, some people pick and choose. They merrily hopscotch their way through the passages of the *Bible*, selecting and neglecting what they feel best suits them.

In reality, it is *all* the word of God—or *none* of it is.

That being said, it is impossible to accept the reality of God, our advocate, without also believing in the existence of a spiritual adversary. If we embrace Jesus for Who He is, we must also understand the presence of His and our spiritual opponent known as Satan or the devil—the father of lies, the great deceiver, the wicked one.

To grasp the promise of a literal place called heaven, we must do the same of a place called hell, for the existence of both is clearly stated in scripture.

This is very basic. *Bible 101*, if you will.

Though God is actively engaged in the lives of those who seek Him, there are occasions when God chooses to be still, to go silent, to become invisible. Eventually, all who live for Him will have their faith tried in various ways such as these.

I certainly have.

You see, long before the days of the Internet and social media, Jesus sent each of us a "friend request," and He has lovingly urged us to accept it.

I did that. At a young age, I accepted Him into my heart, and I understood that decision. But it wasn't until around the time that I graduated from high school and received a new *Bible* from my parents that I began to truly feel God drawing me toward Him in a very real and personal way. It was at that time in my life and for the next several years that I began to really grow spiritually.

However, growth produces growing pains.

Often accompanying true spirituality are periods of spiritual conflict. We can learn these things from a page and from a pulpit, but we don't fully comprehend until we experience them at work in our lives. No one will develop spiritually or grow mature in godliness without facing battles in the unseen realm.

When I was younger, though, I didn't truly know this or have an internal grasp on it. Never did it become a reality to me until the beginning of the year 2006.

I began that year with a devout resolution, with a determination, with a surrendering, with a yielding to God. I wanted to know His definitive will for my life, to be a tool in His hand, and to hear His voice within.

I made myself vulnerable and available by praying that God would use my life to honor Him and to bless others. I wanted my existence and my condition to count for something. Desiring God's plan to unfold and His will to be done, I was open for whatever He wanted.

After several years of growing, I was ready to get going!

If the Good Lord had a job assignment for me, I was prepared to roll up my dangly little sleeves and get to work. That was my desire and my prayer.

But then, something happened; the ringside bell had rung. Though I didn't know what was transpiring in my life, battle between opposing forces became exceptionally real to me.

I was asked to share my testimony at the little church near our home in Pittsburgh. I have already written about how stressful and uncomfortable it was for me to go out and speak in public like that. But it was after that experience—soon after my first speech early in 2006—when it felt like my entire world had tilted in the wrong direction.

Everything appeared to unravel around me.

During that time, God went missing, or so it seemed.

He just disappeared like I thought goodness and mercy had.

Being my first of such experiences, it brought me distress and confusion. I didn't understand what was happening. I just knew something was different, something was wrong. Though I was strong in my faith and had been growing ever closer to God, it seemed He had ducked around a corner and hid Himself.

During that time, suddenly, somehow, from somewhere, a shadow slid in and covered me. It left me feeling alone and forgotten and without meaning or worth.

It didn't make sense that the result of my earnest seeking of direction could leave me feeling so unguided and misplaced.

The silent question was: *What can I do about it?*

For me, the answer was simple. Or, it was simply the only answer I had. There was only one thing to do, just one place to go. Blanketed by darkness, I could do nothing but seek the light.

It was the same logic as that of Saint Peter, I suppose. Recorded in the *Bible* was a time when many turned away from following Jesus, and He asked His twelve apostles if they were going to leave also.

This was Peter's reply:

"Lord, to whom shall we go? You have the words of eternal life. Also we have come to believe and know that You are the Christ, the Son of the living God." John 6:68, 69 (NKJV)

Peter was an insightful man. I followed his example by continually going back to Jesus. Though it seemed He had disappeared, I knew He was the only Truth to Whom I could turn. There was no alternative. There was no other feasible option.

Like I said earlier, you can't go any higher than God.

So, I continued doing what I had known to do—going to church, digging into my *Bible*, and praying.

Still, the warfare within me intensified as I sought Him, and I didn't comprehend what I was going through. In hindsight, I now realize Satan had a hand in it.

It was with good reason that Jesus referred to Satan as the father of lies. That's what he does: he lies, he deceives, he destroys through falsehood, he whispers untruths that can harm us.

The lie that I began to believe was that I was a horrible person.

Because it seemed that I had lost my way and I couldn't feel God's closeness, I began to think that my life had no meaning and that God couldn't possibly love me. His presence had either slipped away, or I had pushed it away. Furthermore, I thought it was gone for good and that it was entirely my fault.

The circumstances around me appeared to support this theory. As mentioned, it was later in that year—around the time of my birthday— when Jade began having seizures, which led to her demise at Christmastime.

But even before then, my life began to feel like it was unraveling. All of 2006 was like that for me, as was a good portion of 2007. Throughout that time, relentless negative thoughts began to weigh on me. For some reason, I felt convinced that I had failed God one too many times, and He decided to wash His hands of me.

I thought He couldn't actually use me as a representative of His kingdom or as a witness of His goodness. There was no way He would bless my endeavors. I just didn't belong.

If anyone had nothing worthwhile to say, it was Amy. Somehow I had become an inadequate square peg hammered with great force into a dark round hole.

It seemed God had stopped listening. Or, maybe He was the One condemning me for my failures. Either way, after years of digging deeper and drawing close to Him, I could no longer feel His presence.

Obviously, I didn't know God's true character at the time. And I wasn't thinking clearly, not understanding that He never speaks to us in a disparaging or disdainful manner. He doesn't condemn. He doesn't accuse. He gently and lovingly nudges us as needed. But I didn't realize that.

If you tally everything up correctly, so far your scorecard should show that, for nearly a year, I felt God had moved away from me. I was struggling with self-doubt and other unhealthy notions. And I lost my service dog.

From there, things got worse.

While I was fresh into the mourning phase over losing Jade, at the end of 2006, there was talk about the Pens possibly relocating to Kansas City, meaning there would be no more Pittsburgh hockey.

As silly as it might sound to most people, this "breaking news" added to my brokenness. Pens hockey was one of very few things that I sincerely enjoyed.

How much is enough?

Where was the bottom?

How much more was I going to lose?

Back then, the Penguins organization hosted a half-hour television show called *Inside Penguins Hockey*. Each episode was taped before a live audience at different locations. The audience could also take part in a questions-and-answers portion of the show and meet the participating players afterwards.

On January 15, 2007, the Pens were scheduled to film a segment at Dick's Sporting Goods in the mall at Robinson, which is only about fifteen miles from us.

Though I had no idea how the show would be set up or what the gathering would fully consist of, I really wanted to be there. I felt it might serve as a pleasant diversion, taking my mind off Jade's death and the hard times that I had been having for nearly the past twelve months.

So, those were my hopes—to be in attendance at *Inside Penguins Hockey* and to be with the players before they'd possibly go on the road for good, heading west, skating into the sunset, going off to reside in Kansas with Dorothy and Toto...leaving Amy in Pittsburgh without Jade.

But, as seemed par for the course, things weren't looking too promising for me on that night.

Neither Cameron nor Myia were able to attend.

Mom didn't want to go.

I couldn't talk Dad into taking me.

But then, thankfully, Candy said she would go, and somewhere in the mix, Dad gave in and agreed to drive us. When we arrived, however, I was faced with a serious problem.

A few of them, actually.

Upon entering the store, I quickly lowered my expectations.

Among other surprises, there were so many people in attendance that you'd think there was rumor of an Elvis sighting in the place. (Yes, Elvis was shopping at Dick's Sporting Goods, apparently.)

In addition to the hockey show, the event would also include three separate autograph sessions. Though the show itself was free, the autograph sessions were not. Each session would have three players. To meet them and get autographs, the fans would have to choose which session they wanted to attend and purchase their ticket accordingly.

This presented a choice—the show or an autograph session.

Either would allow me to meet some of the players, right?

It was a fork in the road at the base of a giant oak tree. But I didn't go left. I didn't go right. Instead, I plowed head-on into the tree trunk. That is to say, as things developed, I didn't choose either. Or, what I did choose would take me nowhere except to the sideline, which was where I began to feel that I belonged.

The rows of people for the first autograph session were so incredibly long that I didn't think it would be a good idea to join in because the wait time would have prevented us from getting a seat for the show.

As it was, the players who I wanted to meet would be in different sessions, which meant it would cost a lot of money to buy tickets for each of those appearances. I didn't have enough. But it wouldn't have mattered because there was no way for me to move from one line to the next, anyhow. I'd have to skip the autograph lines and hope to meet the players after the show was taped.

But I soon found out that that wouldn't happen, either.

Maybe it was due to the overload of people who were there, but, for whatever reason, it was announced that those who would make it into the show would *not* have the opportunity to meet any players afterwards.

With this announcement came the stark realization that I basically had no chance of meeting anyone—definitely not in the show, and probably not in any of the autograph sessions.

With these heartbreaking discoveries, I decided to just sit off to the side and watch the other fans as they met the players and got their autographs. I figured if I could find a place where I wouldn't be a bother to anyone, I could still watch everything and have Candy take pictures for me.

I would settle for that.

But neither of us could see much other than the hind parts of all the fans. When Candy informed me that she wasn't able to get any good shots, my heart sank further.

It was just one more thing among many things. Another boulder heaped upon the ugly mountain that had already been looming over me.

The word dejected doesn't begin to describe how I felt.

With my hopes downgraded to zero, it left me feeling once again that God was nowhere to be found.

All of this had to be a sign; it was further proof that I was an awful person. I didn't deserve to even be there to begin with. I should have been at home mourning Jade, not trying to forget about her if only for a couple of hours.

I shouldn't have been so foolish to show up. Wasn't it bad enough that trouble and disappointment had sought me, found me, and pounced on my back?

Why did I go out looking for more of the same?

Truly, it was going to be a long, dark winter.

Candy had given up an evening with her family. And for what? For nothing. Dad was sitting out in the van, waiting. Also for nothing.

It was best to pack it in, to cut my losses, to point my joystick toward the nearest exit and motor on out of there. The only thing gained was confirmation of how big a fool I was. The lesson learned was that I didn't belong there. I didn't fit in.

My only hope at the moment was that the tears wouldn't fall before I reached the van.

And then, something amazing happened.

Suddenly, out of nowhere, a man approached. He likely either worked at Dick's or for the Pens organization, but I'm not sure. For all I know, he could have been Gabriel or Michael in human disguise.

Or an angel named Clarence.

Whoever he was and whatever his authority, the man offered to escort me to the front, allowing us to bypass the lines and go straight to the players!

I was completely floored by the gesture.

By that time, the first session had ended and the initial set of players had already left, but I was going to have the opportunity to meet the players in the next two sessions!

One of the players that I really wanted to see was Evgeni Malkin, but he was part of the first session. It didn't even matter, though. I had gone from no chance of meeting anyone to the opportunity to meet six of them!

Then, the news got better.

One of the players from an upcoming session couldn't make it for some reason, so Malkin returned to fill his spot. So, I got to meet him, too! When he signed my autograph book, I said, "Thank you."

In his broken English and heavy Russian accent, he said, "Welcome."

Everyone in attendance had been told that they could not ask the players for personal photos. So, what does Candy do? She asks Jordan Staal if I could get my picture with him.

He said, "Sure she can!"

With Jordan Staal

Instead of attending the hockey show, Candy and I had an amazing time in those autograph sessions. And that night turned out to be the best night that I had had in a very long time. The absolute best part was that, of all places, on that night, after all that empty, silent time, God clearly spoke to my heart, right there in Dick's Sporting Goods.

I remember hearing Him whisper to my spirit, reminding me that He *is* listening, He *does* hear me, and He *loves* me! He is constantly setting me up to succeed, not fail. I felt assurance that I *do* belong, and that God *would* use me for His Kingdom, not because He *needs* me, but because He *wants* me! He loves each of us so much that He even cares about the little things that matter to us.

Conditions in my life didn't immediately change for the better after that night, but it was a definite turning point. It offered a glimmer of hope that I would be okay. And I am!

Eventually, the Pens reached a deal to stay in Pittsburgh.

Come summertime, I received Logic.

I then met Eric at church.

On occasion, I still struggle with seasons of worry or fear and with sometimes believing quiet, horrible lies about who I really am. The difference now is that I know who is behind those thoughts, and I remind myself of the night when God orchestrated a chance for me to talk with a group of rugged hockey players.

It's amazing to think that, while I had anticipated greeting the Pens, God showed up—unannounced and unseen—waiting patiently amongst the crowd to greet me!

31

Addressing the Darkness

Hypothetical question: Are birth parents entitled to the first right of refusal or somehow privileged to exercise an option of abandonment? Some folks may wonder how a parent or a set of parents could reject and forsake their own flesh and blood newborn.

While this might sound as worse as it gets in the world, it isn't. I am alive and well. Others have not been so fortunate. Their stories are unbelievably appalling.

How is it that these incidents occur?

How can they possibly exist?

The answer is exceptionally gloomy.

It's the stuff that midnight and shadows are made of. It's the cloak of the lost soul, the misleading guide of spiritual vagrants. It clouds the minds, veils the hearts, and shades the morality of those who are captive to it.

That simple one-word conclusion is "darkness."

It is nighttime's sole ingredient. It is the unseen evil forest, lost to the proverbial trees that it produces, bearing withered leaves and poisonous fruit.

Though it may seem still and empty, darkness is alive with lethal movements, lurking through its own covering to prey upon anyone it can, including precious, innocent lives.

Vastly disturbing is that this deadly, colorless substance resides within nameless strangers and anonymous transients who hunt and troll and prowl in pursuit of young, defenseless targets.

More frightening is that many of these vulnerable and fragile victims are harmed at the hands of those who, by nature and instinct, are supposed to love them without condition and protect them at all cost.

Frequently, they are wronged by those who they know and trust—a relative, a trusted neighbor, a family friend, a babysitter.

Often, the offender is a drunken or deadbeat father.

In the United States alone, statistics show that 2,000 children die each year from abuse and neglect. The news reports read like a fictional horror story, and most reveal the worst possible outcome.

Sadly, and disturbingly, there are many terrible stories such as these—most of which are too upsetting to read about, let alone print in my book.

Here are some real-life, modern-day examples, abbreviated and paraphrased, as a quick but appalling look at the darkness of which I speak:

Monmouth Country, New Jersey – November 2012
    Kids playing in Shark River Park notice a tiny hand sticking out of the water and discover the body of a two-year-old girl strapped securely in her car seat, face down in a stream. Her father had picked her up for a court-approved visit. Instead of returning her to her mother, he had tossed the toddler into the creek and fled to California.

Though many do not end so tragically, all such incidences are equally disturbing. They expose the darkness in which many children are forced to live.

And in an apparent bid for equality and shared notoriety, moms have also become common offenders. According to the Anthropology Association, more than 200 women a year kill their children in the United States. Many others commit unthinkable acts of different kinds.

Dallas, Texas – September 2011
    A young drug addicted mom savagely beats her two-year-old daughter to the brink of death due to frustration with potty training. The punishment involved the child being bitten, kicked in the stomach,

and struck with a milk jug. As an added penalty, the woman then stuck the toddler's hands to the wall with Superglue.

As has forever been the case, there are always the acts of predatory strangers, the haunters and hunters who lurk in the shadows, saturated by the darkness within their own souls. There are also those who fall somewhere between family and stranger, guest and intruder. Disgusting and horrifying offenses have come at their hand as well.

Lucasville, Ohio – May 2013
    A man is executed in the Lucasville prison. Nearly fifteen years prior, he had killed a six-month-old girl—the daughter of his new girlfriend—in the most disgusting of ways; he literally raped the baby until she died. The man claimed that it happened while he was drunk and that he didn't know he was hurting her.

These shocking and senseless occurrences go far beyond the weight and greyness that I experienced in '06 and '07. This is a form of obscurity that is so much worse.

Is it not a clear, luminous snapshot of evil? Is darkness not the central theme, the blind obvious? Is Satan not the root cause? Is this not a product of his blackened hands?

And these are only a few of the many terrible headlines that have surfaced during the writing of my books. Sadly, they stand among countless and continuing others.

How could these things exist if not for deep moral darkness?

How can we be made aware of such atrocities and other horrific, unimaginable deeds and not recognize that this darknesss truly persists?

Who would have thought that it could come in so many shades and varieties? More importantly, is there anything that can be done about it?

Darkness is imbued throughout our society, throughout civilization, worldwide.

Can it be confronted?

Could it possibly be defeated?

Dare we have hope in such austerity?

Do we have a countermeasure?

Is there an answer? Is there an antidote?

Is there a cure?

I believe the answer is a resounding yes!

32

Embracing the Light

Helen Keller once said, "Science may have found a cure for most evils; but it has found no remedy for the worst of them all: the apathy of human beings."

It seems truly difficult to dispute anything stated by such a brilliant and inspiring person as Helen Keller. Though she lived her entire life in silent sightlessness, she exuded a light of wisdom and sensitivity that most of us could never begin to imagine.

But can we truly believe that science has found a cure for most evils? Has it found a cure for even *some* of them?

Surely, darkness exists just as nighttime exists. Evil runs loud and rampant in places where it once quietly tiptoed. It has not been conquered by the efforts of man. Medicine has discovered no healing for it. Science has found no cure.

Still, I believe that, as the darkness abides, a true remedy remains readily available.

As life is the premium choice, the greatest blessing, the ultimate gift, darkness has found a conquering foe in the presence of illumination.

The antidote to blackness, the remedy for shadows, the cure for the destructive forces of darkness is light. Where it shines, darkness withers and scatters and flees in defeat.

Light is what fills people like Eric Fabian, the Band of Brothers, Brett Barry, and so many others.

It is that light shining within individuals who, like my parents, would care for the weak and neglected, the poor and the sick, the discarded and the downtrodden.

It is that light which causes others, like Eric's parents, to move beyond a dismal past and live in such a way that is productive, fruitful, positive, and enriching.

It is that light that creates heroes from the ordinary by instilling in people the willingness to give and serve and reject the selfish trends of pushing and taking.

These individuals walk in the light of day rather than lurking in the slippery shadows of darkness.

They offer help to those who have been harmed.

They promote love where others have produced hate.

It is that light—not the mere passing of time—that heals our wounds.

It is that light which gives us hope and strength and courage.

It opens the eyes of our understanding, causing us to see truth and reality as it accurately exists. Ultimately, it is that light which dispels the darkness around us.

Even a faint amount can pierce the darkest of nights. It is ever present, shining in an assortment of places and at various lumens.

A timely illustration of this light was given to us long ago in the Middle East. I'm sure we're all familiar with the main character.

He was a nameless man dubbed "the Good Samaritan."

You may or may not know the details of the story.

If you are among the "may-nots," I will provide a brief overview. Since we covered some Greek in my first book, it only seems fitting to offer something in the Hebrew category, right?

If you'd like to read the story for yourself, it's found in the *Bible*—in the Tenth chapter of Luke's gospel. It's there for safekeeping and for future reading. More than that, it's there as a pattern for us to follow. Many have done so.

It all started when a self-righteous and arrogant man comes to Jesus and asks what he must do in order to go to heaven. Jesus turns it back on him by asking, *"What do the scriptures say to do?"*

The man says, *"You shall love the Lord your God with all your heart, and with all your soul, and with all your strength, and with all your mind, and love your neighbor as yourself."*

Jesus replies, *"You have answered correctly. Do these things, and you will have eternal life."*

Looking for a quick exit or some sort of loophole, the man smugly asks, *"And who is my neighbor?"*

Jesus answers with a parable about a man traveling to the city of Jericho. Please, allow me to paraphrase:

> *On the way to Jericho, thieves jump the traveler and rob him of everything he has, including the clothes on his back. They beat the man half dead, and they flee.*
>
> *Sometime later, a devout religious man walks by and sees the bloody victim lying on the roadside. He doesn't want to be bothered, so he crosses the road and goes on his way.*
>
> *Another esteemed official walks by and does the same thing, literally following in the footsteps of the uncaring religious man.*
>
> *The robbery victim is left bleeding and dying.*
>
> *Finally, an unknown traveler approaches. He is a stranger, someone who is considered an outcast or an enemy because he is from Samaria.*
>
> *This traveler sees the injured man and has compassion for him. He immediately tends to his needs by giving him medicine and by bandaging his wounds. The Samaritan then lifts the man onto his own donkey and takes him to a lodge and continues to look after him throughout the night.*
>
> *Before leaving the next morning, the Samaritan pays for the man's room and leaves extra money with the clerk. He also requests that the injured man be taken care of. Knowing he would be passing through again, the Samaritan promises that, if the money he left was not sufficient to fully cover the man's care, he would pay the difference when he returned.*

Jesus finishes the story by asking, *"Which of the men was a neighbor to the man?"*

The religious man replies, *"I suppose it was the one who had mercy on him."*

Jesus then instructs the man to *"Go, and do likewise."*

Nice story, huh?

Heartwarming, isn't it?

Trust me; I didn't make it up.

I don't write fiction.

I'm just not that imaginative.

But that story serves as a guideline for us to follow. Many have done so.

Lights have shined far above and well beyond what we have known or imagined.

Here are some real-life, modern-day examples, also abbreviated and paraphrased:

Toronto, Ontario – June 2013

While on a cross-country Canadian tour, a seventy-seven-year-old Ohio man and his wife has just exited a restaurant where they had eaten. Walking past a construction scaffold, the man stumbles on the sidewalk and falls. Before he hits the ground, a protrusion sticking out from the scaffold slices the man's neck.

Having witnessed the horrible ordeal, the owner of the restaurant and a respected customer rush outside to assist the man. While waiting for medical help to arrive, the restaurant patron cradles the man's head and applies hand pressure to the wound to minimize the bleeding.

When the injured man asks the name of the gentleman who was tending to him, the man simply offers his first name. After the elderly man is professionally treated and is on his way to recovery, he learns the identity of the fellow customer who helped him. To his surprise, it was a successful Hollywood actor.

The elderly man said, "I'd like to thank the gentleman."

A good deed, a random display of kindness, or an act of mercy: sometimes that's all that's needed to make a lasting difference.

Boston, Massachusetts – April 2013

A woman running the 26.2-mile Boston Marathon is only half a mile from finishing the race when two successive explosions go off near the finish line.

The marathon is immediately stopped as chaos breaks out. The woman is confused as to what is happening. The only thing she is sure of is that she will not be allowed to complete the race.

Wandering in shock near the finish line, the woman is crying. A passing couple stops to comfort her. The man is a runner who had finished the race about thirty minutes earlier. The woman walking with him is his wife.

Stirred with compassion, the runner's wife takes the space tent off her husband and wraps it around the woman. She asks if she is okay and if she knows where her family is.

The female runner states that she does know where they are and that she would be alright.

The man then asks if she had finished the marathon.

The woman shakes her head no.

He tells her, "You are a finisher in my eyes."

In a move that is as shocking as the explosions, the man removes his race medal from around his neck and places it on hers. "You deserve it," he says.

Bursting with sobs, the woman is barely able to say, "thank you."

Later, she posts her story on the Internet in hopes of locating the couple.

In time, the male runner is identified by the news media. He is a forty-six-year-old from Sitka, Alaska. When an Alaskan radio station interviews him and his wife, the man shares his perspective:

"There were all these thousands of runners with their running bibs, but none of them were wearing medals because they never finished," he said. "Many of them were at mile twenty-five, twenty-six when, all of a sudden, they couldn't run anymore because of what had happened."

He continues. "We were with a gal who was crying. She didn't finish the race. I just gave her my medal, my race medal because I finished and got my medal, and she didn't finish, and she deserved a medal."

The female runner tells media outlets that the kind gesture helped her believe that "even though such a terrible thing had happened, everything was going to be okay."

Many such stories can be found—stories of compassion, stories of sacrifice, stories of selfless giving. All are inspiring. Each one emits light. And they offer a small glimpse of the character of God.

God is good. (reference - Psalm 136:1)

God is love. (1 John 4:8 KJV)

God is merciful. (Deuteronomy 4:31 NKJV)

God is gracious and full of compassion. (reference - Psalm 145:8)

God is light, and in him is no darkness at all. (1 John 1:5 KJV)

Countless caring individuals have ventured into the unknown or rushed into danger to assist others, even complete strangers. They did so with everything to lose and nothing to gain except for that which benefits their "neighbor."

These are demonstrations of empathy and expressions of self-denial. They are ingredients of light, components of wholesomeness, elements of that which is truly good. They are random samplings that offer enrichment. Scattered displays that inspire and bring hope. All were from regular, everyday people who were willing to get involved.

Earlier in this book, Eric told you about the Robison's safe water project for children in Africa. I also shared my story of incredible thirst, as my body craved much-needed hydration.

But those stories and situations are universal.

Many who are around us thirst spiritually. They are barren souls longing to be satisfied. You might be the person to lead them to water, to help quench their thirst.

As Jesus is light, He is also a well of living water. He said if we drink from His well, we will never thirst again. (reference - John 4:14)

Also, if we drink from that well, we will have something to offer others—something of meaning, something of substance, something that is eternal.

The late Christian singer/songwriter/musician Rich Mullins once said, "I want to be one of those people for someone else. I think there can't be any greater joy in life than knowing that someone else's life is richer because you lived."

Mr. Mullins truly had something to offer, and he gave it passionately, without regret or reservation, because he drank from the well of life. He walked in righteousness. And he embraced the light of God.

Can we possibly be content with settling for anything less?

33

So, Who Am I?

I f you've stayed with me and have read to this page without skipping ahead, you are now acquainted with my life as it has been lived thus far, in real-time and in full color.

Perhaps I have answered the silent and obvious question: *What is it like to have been born without arms and legs?*

Either way, I hope our meeting has been a pleasant one for you.

Hopefully, I've gained you as a friend.

But who am I, really?

To answer that question, a portion of my response would have to include who I am *not*, or maybe *what* I am not.

While I am unmistakably the recipient and rightful owner of what is considered an extremely rare birth defect, I am not defective.

I am not remanufactured, refurbished, or recycled.

I am not an accidental shipment of damaged goods.

Not a bookend, not a doorstop, not a shortstop, not a speed bump.

I am not a tabloid story.

Nor am I a Muppet or a Minion or a human emoticon.

Not a sprig or a sprout.

I am not a creationism experiment gone badly.

I am not a partly assembled assortment of miscellaneous pieces.

I am not a human abbreviation or the product of an erroneous measurement.

I am nothing catastrophic and nothing diminished.

I am not a throw pillow. Not a knick-knack. Not a centerpiece. Not a hood ornament or a human bowling pin. And as much as I love Christmas, I am not a tree topper.

So, who am I?

Foremost, I believe, unequivocally, that I am a child of God. I am someone who is confident that God has fashioned me, and I am confident that He did so without error or miscalculation.

He shook the box. He checked the invoice. There were no pieces left over. No missing contents or lack of necessary components. There were no quality control issues. I contain no suspect parts.

I have no inventory shortage.

No further assembly is required.

Of greater importance is to realize that no one is responsible for my birth condition. No one is to blame.

As for the "Why me?" question, I have never asked it other than in reference to the many blessings that have come my way.

God is my Creator. Period. End of story. Final answer.

There was no sleeping at the wheel or dozing at the controls. Nothing has slipped past Him. He encounters no surprises. He is never caught unknowing. He is never unaware.

At the start of each day, throughout its duration, and in the hours of darkness, I am not a victim. I am me without mistake. I am me as God intended. He knew me before I took my first breath. He lovingly whispered my name.

So, who am I?

I am a woman who loves God, a woman who loves light and life.

Made in Pittsburgh, I am stamped with time, but sealed for eternity.

No longer a codename, I am Amy, without regret.

I am Amy, unashamed.

Yet, none of that means a whole lot, does it? It's okay to agree because that isn't what I want most to leave with you. That isn't today's curriculum or my overall hypothesis. Nor is it the heart of my testimony.

A songwriter named Harlan Howard once said, "Music is about three chords and the truth."

We might want to consult Brett Barry about that.

Myself, I've never played a chord or composed any music, and I have no experience with songwriting. But comparatively, what can be said of printed literature? How would we define a book of personal memoirs or delineate an autobiographical manuscript?

More specifically, what is this particular book all about?

What is its actual purpose? What is my message?

For one thing, I'd like for you to see the similarities between us, to identify our commonalities, to draw a parallel line between you and me.

By that, I mean we all possess a label of distinction.

We wear an invisible badge of uniqueness.

I do, and you do.

Of course, when you look at me, you see the obvious. Yet, many who are "whole" on the outside have a "hole," on the inside. What they are missing isn't so easily noticed.

It might be self-worth, or direction, or confidence. Maybe it's a sense of purpose, or the simple ability to enjoy life and appreciate what they have. They might even completely dislike themselves for whatever reason.

Many are filled with emptiness, carrying a hidden void, an internal vacancy that they often attempt to plug in ways and with means that were never intended. Sometimes they cover it with harmful substance or destructive activities.

Maybe that's you, maybe it isn't.

Whether it is or not, we all share a common bond.

Our Declaration of Independence insists, *"All men are created equal and endowed by their Creator..."*

I believe that. But I prefer God's wordsmanship. He invented the concept. He originated the phrase. I like His rendering better. The *Bible* says that we are *"fearfully and wonderfully made."*

None of us are accidents.

None are aberrations of God, man, science, or otherwise.

Regardless of our condition or view of self, we are all intricate and priceless formations. Each of us was intelligently designed, intentionally made, and individually wrapped.

To God and by Him, we are handcrafted pieces of art. We are earthen treasures. We were purposely created, and each of our lives holds a significant purpose.

All lives matter!

What I desire for you to take hold of is far beyond the measurements and meagerness of my own being. It is something much greater than who I am and who you are.

I wish to offer you more than an explanation for why I am publicly confined to a wheelchair or why I cannot wave hello when you pass me in a shopping mall.

What I aspire for you to grasp is so amazing and yet so completely attainable.

It is bigger than me.

It is higher than you.

And yet, it is right at your fingertips.

It is so mindboggling, yet so simple.

And it is so incredibly real.

In addition to drawing a line of commonality between us, I want to connect the dots between you and God. If that link has already been made, I wish to see those dots become more boldly defined and transitioned into a thick, solid cord that tethers you to His very heart.

My desire is for you to realize that—no matter who you are—a good and loving Creator has formed you. My message is that your life has a purpose. There is significance and a great value invested inside of you from birth.

To know that, to understand it, to believe it is the difference between a fulfilled life and an empty existence. It is an invisible substance that offers a peaceful present and a successful future.

None of it is based on what others say, what they think about you, or what they do. It's up to you. It's between you and God.

If my future were dependent upon how others saw me, I would have a much different reality. Instead, I'm learning to view myself as God sees me. It is my desire for you to do the same for yourself.

So, who am I?

I am someone who believes there is good in people. We find that in some of the previous stories of heroism and selfless giving. Yet, the greater good, the ultimate light, the culmination of all things kind and caring and wholesome is God.

We may try to be good on our own, and we can even do good things, but "good" is not good enough.

There are no accomplishments listed as a prerequisite to heaven. Heroism isn't a requirement. You can't do enough good to earn God's favor.

Can't jump high enough.

Can't walk far enough.

Doing good works or daring deeds doesn't earn us acceptance or grant us entrance. Remember, the story of the Good Samaritan begins with the command to love God and to love others.

These attributes lend themselves to good works, but good works alone won't cut it. Also, there is no visible measuring stick provided in determining how much "goodness" we need.

Doesn't that seem kind of cruel?

Well, I suppose it would be if our eternal salvation was solely based on our earthly goodness. As it turns out, we do have a reliable measuring stick, but it doesn't measure human works or acts of kindness. And it isn't the typical twelve-inch ruler or the yardstick type.

The measuring sticks we were given consist of two pieces, made of heavy splintered wood, bisecting at ninety-degree angles. The positioning of these "sticks" creates the form of a cross. That cross connects and gages our heart to God's.

Who am I?

I am someone who firmly stands at the foot of that cross. I measure myself by what it represents and by the message it carries.

I have embraced that cross, but not merely the symbol of it; I have acknowledged and received the One Who willingly laid His life upon it.

I know firsthand, and I know *without* hands, God is a good and loving God. I have sampled His kindness, experienced His mercy, and accepted His grace. I have drunk of His living water and tasted His sweetness.

I am a woman who is eternally held in unseen arms, enveloped by a majestic God Whose reach is extended to all. I am kept by a loving Savior. He is as real to me as life itself, the benefits of which are yet to be fully realized.

In *Unseen Arms*, Mom wrote how she had prayed for me as a baby, that I'd somehow walk someday. She also says that prayer was answered in my waddling about on the duck feet and in my ability to limp around on my hips.

Perhaps so. But I don't believe God is finished answering that prayer.

We have not yet seen what He has in store.

For the *Bible* declares:

No eye has seen,
no ear has heard,
no mind has conceived
what God has prepared for those who love him.
I Corinthians 2:9 (NIV)

Please, write that down, read it often, or otherwise commit it to memory.

Within my heart of hearts, I know there will come a day when, instead of putting on artificial limbs, I will slip into an entirely new body, in a place where prosthetics are banished and wheelchairs are nonexistent.

It is a land that contains no deformities or affliction. It knows no sickness or disease. It allows no pain or suffering. Death is obsolete there, and all darkness is superseded by glorious light.

In that place, I will run—yes, RUN—across rolling hills and dash through flourishing meadows, and I will do so on two fully developed legs.

There in the plush, celestial field, I will throw my arms—my two complete and healthy arms—around the neck of my Lord and Savior!

It is my earnest desire that you and I will meet there and that we will abide with Him forever!

34

Who Are You?

To share my story is a privilege. For you to read it through, I'm honored. But as stated, this book really isn't about me. Telling my story for the sake of telling it was never my intention; otherwise, I would have never written it.

Not only did various people predict that I'd someday write a book, for years my family members and friends urged me to write one. But I wanted nothing to do with the idea.

That said, my book—both of my books—are about so much more than a limbless thirty-two-inch female from Pittsburgh named Amy.

My books are about God's involvement in human lives.

In part, this book is about you.

Above that which is entertaining, nonsensical, or funny, beyond anything useful, enlightening, or informative, my books are intended to provide inspiration, hope, encouragement, and maybe some guidance in helping you look a little closer at who you are.

Regardless of what you see outwardly, I'm a whole person. Are you? Are you fulfilled? Are you whole on the inside, or do you have a hole on the inside?

Who are you?

What do you believe?

Why do you believe it?

Are you living accordingly?

Somewhere in time, if you haven't already, I hope you will face the realization that you are created by God and born for a purpose. I want you to know that you have great worth. You are pricelessly valued.

I also aspire for you to understand that your worth is not defined by the world's opinion. What people say and what God says is often completely opposite. Your life is significant. It has God-given purpose and holds unlimited potential.

It may not be that which we have envisioned for ourselves or what others have predicted for us, but God has a plan for each of our lives.

When you turn the final page and tuck this book on the shelf, it doesn't matter if you remember me or if you forget me. It's not important that you know who I am. What is most essential is that you know yourself.

For us to know ourselves, it is imperative that we settle our internal issues and eternal questions. We must know what we believe and why we believe it. We must also understand where we stand. And it is vital to know where we are going, what direction we are headed.

So, the question I must ask is, "Who are you?"

To be the type of person who would read such a book as this, you are probably not someone who can personally relate to the deep, disturbing darkness described in Chapter Thirty-One.

However, do you feel like you might be lost in a grey area? Are you caught in a vacuum, trapped in a void, stuck in a barren land? Betrayed or abandoned perhaps?

How you describe your past experiences or current situation isn't of utmost importance. What you do about it is.

At the end of the day—at the end of *all* days—it comes down to our choices.

Where do we stand with God?

What do we do?

Where do we go?

How do we treat others?

Do you find a reflection of yourself in any of the Good Samaritan stories? Frankly, it doesn't matter if you do or not. You see, there is a brighter light than that of moral heroism or modern-day servitude.

There are things that extend beyond the borders of that which is newsworthy; they are the everyday, steady actions that guide us. They are the components that make up our true character—the way we are when we are alone and when no one is looking.

You may not have assisted a foreign traveler or given a prized possession to a stranger. That's okay.

But who are you?

What is really on the inside?

Unfortunately, people want to be different from who they are or from who they were intended to be. Everyone wants to be a fifth grader. Or, everyone wants to be smarter than a millionaire.

But who are you in God's eyes?

Who does He want you to be?

As stated earlier, it is oftentimes the smallest of things that matter most, and certainly the inner, unseen things. The external things can fool us. They might even lead us astray.

Feet can take us places we maybe ought not to go. Hands can allow us the ability to touch things we shouldn't.

Consider this: if I had been born a "full-figured" girl, if I was whole and even perfect in body, my birth parents likely would have kept me.

Remember, they left me because of my missing limbs.

So, what if I would have had those limbs? What would I be like if they had kept me and raised me? There's a good chance my life would not be fulfilling or meaningful.

Obviously, I would have grown up in a different home, in a different environment, under a different set of guidelines and values. Maybe those things would have been destructive to me in the long run, possibly for eternity.

In the pages of my introduction, I mentioned a few friends that I was enthused about introducing. You've met Logic, Eric, Brett, and several other wonderful individuals, but there remains another who is most special to me. This friend is Jesus Christ. He is *Emmanuel, which being interpreted is, God with us.* (Matthew 1:23 KJV) He is a hero of extreme magnitudes. He is the One that I want you to know and remember at the close of this book.

Also in my introduction, I asked you to come along with me, "right where you am and just how you is." Though it was said in a playful and lighthearted fashion, that is precisely how we come to Jesus.

Remember, there are no prerequisites. There are no practice runs or warm-up exercises. No religious rites to be performed. We just come to Him, lost, broken, and empty. We come with the hole and allow Him to fill it. We bring him our darkness or our thirst. He gives us light and living water.

These are the things you must remember.

An astute but unaccredited person once said, "If you meet me and forget me, you've lost nothing. If you meet Jesus Christ and forget Him, you've lost everything."

Have you met Him? Do you truly know Him?

That's what this book is about. That's what Amy Brooks is all about. My desire is to point you to Jesus, that you might know Him, unforgettably and eternally.

He is the true shining light in an ever-darkening world.

Exposure to Him, introduction to that light, means clear visibility and access to the goodness contained within it. God is that light.

As for the good in people, that's where it comes from. If it's in you, if it's in me, God put it there.

Conversely, if we lend ourselves to darkness, we risk becoming a part of it, joining forces at any level with the slithering shadows of apathy, selfishness, greed, or things that are so much worse.

The message I hope to convey is that of the goodness of God and what He has to so freely offer. And the only true way to know Him is through the sacrifice of His Son, Jesus Christ.

You may not study Greek words like Tetraphocomelia or Hebrew parables like that of the Good Samaritan. You may not attend classes or invest time toward academic enrichment or social learning.

Maybe you're not a person of faith, a *Bible* reader, or someone who is considered "spiritually seeking." But this does not change truth.

God is still God whether we believe Him or not. His light is forever shining, and nothing can diminish it. As declared in the *Bible*—some of which I have already listed—a few but very clear characteristics of God are thus:

God is good. God is love. God is merciful. God is gracious. God is full of compassion. God is true. God is Holy. God is eternal. God is forgiving. God is light. God cannot lie. God never changes.

I hope you make a note of those things.

Eventually, we will all be tested on it.

Not on paper, but in real life. Not with a No. 2 pencil, but with the choices we make and with how we use the tools, the talents, and the information we've been given.

These tests will challenge what we know and will confront the core of our beliefs. They are tests that none can afford to fail.

You can't, and I can't.

Seeing me in my limbless condition, I hope you realize that I *do* have arms—unseen arms—that are ever extended to God's welcoming embrace. He, too, has unseen arms, fully extended to each of us. In good experiences and bad, in times of joy and suffering, in confidence and hopelessness, in strength and in weakness, in the light of day and through the shadow of darkness, His loving arms are reaching out for you.

But what does it say? "The word is near you; it is in your mouth and in your heart," that is, the word of faith we are proclaiming:

That if you confess with your mouth, "Jesus is Lord," and believe in your heart that God raised him from the dead, you will be saved.

For it is with your heart that you believe and are justified, and it is with your mouth that you confess and are saved.

As the Scripture says, "Anyone who trusts in him will never be put to shame."

For there is no difference between Jew and Gentile—the same Lord is Lord of all and richly blesses all who call on him,

for, "Everyone who calls on the name of the Lord will be saved."

Romans 10:8-13 (NIV)

Acknowledgments

from Amy

The acknowledgements section, for me, is the hardest part of the book. Not because I have no one to acknowledge or be thankful for, but because I have SO MANY to be thankful for. No amount of words could ever adequately describe what each of them mean to me.

Having said that, first and foremost, my whole heart goes to my Lord and Savior, Jesus Christ. It is in Him that I have life and because of Him that I have a future.

Thank you, Mom and Dad, for literally being my hands and feet, selflessly offering them whenever I'm in need. Mom, thank you for laughing with me—even those times when you know you shouldn't, but you do it anyway. It keeps me going. And for being my trusted source for spiritual counsel. Dad, for being a Godly example of how a father loves his children and a husband loves his wife. Love yinz both!

A HUGE thank you to my entire family, my village people. It truly does take a village to keep this girl going and you always rise to the occasion!

Jeff, thank you for dedicating so much time and effort to these books. For having a vision and seeing it through. Giving it your all, not settling for anything less than perfect. Miss Ginny, thank you for placing your husband on part-time loan over the past four and a half years. A special thanks to Miss Tamara for your expertise in the English language and to the rest of the Ferris clan for allowing me to be a "little" part of your family.

To the churches, schools, and other venues who, over the past year and a half, have allowed me to share the story God gave me...thank you.

Mark, thank you for being the first to believe I could!

Mr. John Paul Owles and Joshua Tree Publishing, thank you for believing in me. Because of you, I have been able to share with hundreds, and even thousands of people, the story God blessed me with.

Brett, thank you for not only agreeing to team up with Jeff for my song, but for going that extra mile and a half to make it extra special. It has been such a blessing to me. On those days when I struggle a little, your words remind me that there are unseen arms always holding me.

Alex, I am honored to be part of the team at SteelGate Studio. Thank you for helping to make my dreams of being an artist come true. This last year has been a whirlwind full of new-found knowledge and lots of adventure. I love being the "Oracle" of SteelGate.

Eric, my favorite creep—my life drastically changed the day I met you...and all for the better. You started my family and me on this crazy new adventure in life, and all along the way you have been there through the good, the bad, and everything in between. Thank you for seeing in me what I could never see myself

Thank you to my favorite Band of Brothers. Your big hearts always lead you to those in need.

Acknowledgments

from Jeff

Like Amy, the list of people I could thank is endless. Whether they have supported my writing or had a positive impact on my life in general, each is greatly valued and worthy of mention.

Going back to 1974 and seventh grade, I want to thank Rob for sharing his faith and leading me to Christ.

Ginny, how appropriate it was that Rob and I were together when I met you, four years later. Since then, you have brought me complete fulfillment. Every day, for thirty-three years, you have been an amazing, loving wife and a godly, selfless woman. And every day, for thirty-three years, I have been thankful. In support of my writing sessions, you willingly forfeited much of our time together, giving me up to a computer for more hours than either of us could ever keep track of. My love for you continues to grow.

Tamara, Vanessa, and Jason, each of you amaze and inspire me in your own way. You are awesome, caring, responsible individuals, and you are truly making a difference in the world.

To "Alligator Stevie" and my ladybug, Natalie: being a grandpa is so much fun because of you. I live for your hugs and smiles.

Thank you to my relatives and friends, near and far, to Pastor Steve and my church family at Central Park Congregational, and all others who have supported *Unseen Arms*.

John and Robin at Pathway, I am honored that you find my articles print worthy. I appreciate your grace and patience when I don't have time to submit anything or when I fail to make a deadline. Thank you for investing in my growth as a writer.

Brett, thank you for ministering to my home, for so many years, through your incredible music. You have continually reminded me that following Jesus is an adventure of a lifetime.

Eric, you are the one who got all of this off the ground. I am pleased to know you.

Mr. Owles, I value your insight and wisdom. I am looking forward to another of our rare but lengthy conversations.

Rich and Janet, thank you for having us into your home and for extending such hospitality. (Janet, when this all began—on March 6, 2011, to be exact—you joked that there wasn't much in Amy's life to write about. I won't say I told you so, but apparently we did manage to scrounge up enough material to write a "whole book." And it seems we deleted half as much.)

Amy, I am grateful to live in a country where the unforeseen, the unusual, and even the impossible can happen—especially if God is in our lives. Where else can an autoworker pursue a literary interest and become a published writer? And with so many credited authors and capable journalists on the planet, who else but Amy Brooks would agree to have her memoires ghosted by a tool and die maker?

Working with you, a skilled artist, has prompted me to reach deeper into the treasure chest of creativity. Thank you for that and for tolerating my sleep deprived ideas. (Though we may have colored outside the lines a little, I think we got away with it.) This entire project has been an unbelievable journey. I am convinced God has blessed it and will continue to do so. Our work together, over these past years, has been an extremely pleasant experience for me. I am excited about the things that are happening for you and eager to see what God has waiting behind door number two...and three...and four...

I am honored to know you and blessed to call you my friend. Never did we drop the gloves on each other! Who would have guessed that a Pens fan and a Wings fan could get along so well?

About the Authors

Amy Brooks is a joyful, exuberant, and faithful Christian whose vision is to glorify Jesus Christ by testifying to the unbeliever of His saving grace and by bringing encouragement to those who already know Him. Her writing honors her adoptive family and their unconditional love for her.

Jeff Ferris began pursuing a biographical career in August 2006, at the age of forty-four. This is his third published book and second with Amy Brooks. Jeff is a contributing writer for Pathway Christian Newspaper, a print publication in Toledo, Ohio that can also be read online at pathwaycn.com.

Photo Credits:

Alex Jones: AlexJonesPhotography.com
Photos: Cover and Pages 10, 156, 157

Kristi Jan Hoover: KristiJanHoover.com
Photos: Pages 3, 75, 150

Michael Gianechini: GandGStudio.com
Photo: Page 154

Skylar Kaylan: SkylarKaylyn.com
Jeff's Bio Photo

For more information, visit AmyBrooks.org

CPSIA information can be obtained
at www.ICGtesting.com
Printed in the USA
FFOW04n1226020216
21052FF

9 781941 049389